Prayer
Simplified

PRAYER
SIMPLIFIED

ADETONA SAMUEL

authorHOUSE®

AuthorHouse™
1663 Liberty Drive
Bloomington, IN 47403
www.authorhouse.com
Phone: 1-800-839-8640

First published by AuthorHouse   02/15/2012

ISBN: 978-1-4678-8927-8 (sc)
ISBN: 978-1-4678-8928-5 (ebk)

Printed in the United States of America

For all feedback to the author:
prayersimplified@gmail.com

CONTENTS

DEDICATION

To God the Father, to whom all flesh shall come

To God the Son, the Great High Priest

To God the Holy Spirit, the Helper of our infirmities

To Dad, Rev E.A. Adetona, who led me to Christ

To my wife, Wumi Adetona, for being very patient and understanding

To all my friends and Family, for their support.

ACKNOWLEDGEMENT

All the glory and praise to God for the completion and the publication of this book. Appreciation goes to the following people that helped in proof reading the book and also for their input—Rev. E.A. Adetona, Venerable Dr. Dadeolu Sadare, Mrs. Yemi Adeyemo, Mr. Dele Layioye, Lanre Alao-Samson and Wumi Adetona.

Also, thanks for the encouragement received from Samson Amu and Kenneth Igiri.

FORWARD

This book, *PRAYER SIMPLIFIED* written by our beloved, Adetona Samuel , will be a good guide for every child of God who desires to know more about prayers.

The church today is facing some problems of misguided forms and approaches to effective prayers caused by some prayer leaders who do not have any clear idea about how to pray, what to pray for and modalities for rightful, effective and acceptable prayers.

Therefore, I commend our Adetona for sparing the time to do the research work which has helped him put together the contents of this book - *PRAYER SIMPLIFIED*. And I also recommend this book to every child of God and especially those who may be having problems on the way to acceptable and effective prayer guide.

May the LORD continue to guide us with the power of His Holy Spirit. Amen.

Ven. S. ADE GEORGE
Archdeacon,
IKORODU ARCHDEACONRY,
Diocese of Lagos West (Anglican Communion).
NIGERIA.

AUTHOR'S NOTE

The aim of this book is to keep readers in the know of what prayer is and keep its many facets as SIMPLE as possible. It is also written to fuel the prayer life of Christians (new converts and nominal) having challenges with prayers. All broad topics can be made simple if they are broken down into sub topics or items. Also there are many great prayer legends but none became great in prayer suddenly, it happened by gradual steps as they understood the basics of prayers and built upon the foundation they know. Prayer becomes simple as we know the basics and put what we know into practice over a period of time. Prayer as a topic is inexhaustible as the learning process is continuous.

Prayer can sometimes be abused as well as under utilised. This book helps put issues in the right perspectives.

This book is a condensation of over fifteen years of lessons learnt during personal prayers. It is broken into 30 topics. To get the best from this book, it is strongly recommended that you read a topic daily. You read leisurely and meditatively along with the Bible. After reading the book once, you may start over and over again. I hope you find this material practically helpful for your prayer life.

Knowledge is progressive, there is room to build on what is written here. Therefore, I have included the phrase "LOTS MORE" after highlighting some points on some topics.

May your understanding of prayers be broadened and deepened. May the spirit of prayer be poured powerfully on you as you go through this book.

Humbly yours,

ADETONA SAMUEL.

January, 2012.

INTRODUCTION

PRAYER

Prayer is the act of communication between GOD (CREATOR) and man (CREATURE). Prayer is a dialogue, a two way communication. It is a conversation—talking to God and God talking back.

You can pray anytime, anywhere but not anyhow. It is however an added advantage to have a specific place and time to meet with Him (God) who directs the affairs of the universe. Prayer should also be well ordered. Prayer is one of the top spiritual disciplines.

There are different forms of prayers namely supplication, petition, intercession, praise, worship, thanksgiving and warfare or deliverance prayers. It is good that the believer develops to the extent that he is only a prayer away from the all-knowing and all-hearing God.

Jesus is accustomed to praying (*Mark 1:35; 6:46; Luke 21:37*). Daniel prayed thrice daily (*Daniel 6:10*) despite being a vice-president; his secular responsibilities did not suffer because he had three friends who supported him administratively.

Paul is just a praying brother (*1 Corinthians. 14:18*). The apostles were noted for their prayers; (*Acts 1:14; 2:1; 3:1; 4:31; 6:4; 7:59; 8:15; 9:17; 10:9; 12:5; 13:3,* etc.) no wonder they were said to have turned the world upside down.

Prayer is powerful. Prayer moves 'mountains' regardless of the size, position or duration of stay of the mountain. Prayer brings refreshment. A prayer culture is a very good form of investment—short term and long term. Prayer brings deliverance. Prayer does what the natural man cannot do.

There is no communication company that is able to link the earth (realm of the physical) with God (realm of the true spiritual), but by prayer, it is a great possibility. Either you shout (speak out loud, the prayers of Jesus in *John 17* would not be recorded if Jesus was not audible) or speak gently or the lips just move (Hannah in *1 Samuel 1:13*), which is all subject to the temperament of the person praying which of course should be spirit regulated. A praying man can never live a frustrated life—He will discover purpose. Prayer increases the anointing of God on believers. Prayer is a good weapon ('incantation") against the hosts of hell.

It is important to start the day with prayer and also wind up with prayer. Prayer tends to bring all other weapons of warfare (*Ephesians 6:11-18*) into harmony. Just start praying even when you lack what to say—keep telling God what He is to you. Sometimes when you lack what to say, then keep quiet because God might also want to say something. Be very sincere. Do not impress God with the best of words you think is in the dictionary. Just let your heart be turned away from the natural into the supernatural, and then the supernatural will respond and surpass the result of the natural.

Prayer makes possible the connection to the servers in heaven (*Ephesians 1:3*) and there is access to download 'programs' such as joy, love, peace, knowledge, ideas, mercy, favour, forgiveness, long life, healing, good health, good partner, good home, skills, spiritual gifts, wisdom, finances, understanding, divine connections, jobs, contracts, promotion and lots more. A consistently praying man develops to being a disciplined man. He is also built up to receiving heaven's resources and direction at regular intervals.

Quality prayers keep you on top of any situation. Quality prayers—not just display of words—can bring you out of poverty, can fix marital problems, can give you wisdom that is not taught in the four walls of the school (*James 1:5*), it makes the down trodden to be set on high (*1 Chronicles 4: 9-10*), can reverse medical science verdict, can do more than your skills, gifts and talents. Something things would not happen until we pray.

Praying daily helps you develop a good detection mechanism before danger is fully blown. If you pray regularly in your closest, then you just take authority in the open and things will happen. The best way to learn how to pray is to start praying. Prayer becomes easy if you are engrafted in God's word and also know how to worship Him.

You can stand to pray, lay to pray, walk to pray, knee to pray, lift up your hands or take any posture as long as your heart is tuned and you got none to impress. Prayer should be accompanied with fasting (at least once a week) for more effectiveness. Prayer is also a form of service to God (*Luke 2:37*). Sin however brings about a breakdown in communication between the realm of the tangible and the intangible.

ONE

WHOM TO PRAY TO

PRAYERS BY CHRISTIANS

All Christians should direct all their prayers to GOD because He is the CREATOR of all mankind. People often pray to other gods but the Christian prays to the only true and ever living GOD. To Him will all flesh come (*Psalm 65:2*). All things are open to Him whom we must give account.

All other gods are lesser gods and the works of men, there is non beside Him and He does not share His glory with any because He is a JEALOUS GOD (*Exodus 20:5*).

God is tripartite in nature which is referred to as the Trinity. The Trinity consists of God the Father, God the Son and God the Holy Spirit. These three parts make up the GOD HEAD. Each of the Trinity has their place in the prayer life of the believer. The distinction of their functions can not be adequately described in books because there are some issues about prayers that can not be known by EXPLANATIONS but through personal REVELATION to the believer. As one develops a prayer life, one would understand the distinct functions of each in very clear terms.

PRAYERS BY NON CHRISTIANS

Sometimes, people (non Christians) pray to God without really knowing Him and He answers. God answers them based on the fact that He is the creator of all mankind.

Some people pray to God for healing while they do not yet know Him nor please Him, yet in His infinite mercy, God responds to their cry.

Some unbelievers just obey part of God's principles and because God is faithful to His word, He hears them also. Some unbelievers have insight into what God wants to do. For example, God revealed to King Pharaoh what He intended to do pertaining to famine in the land of Egypt.

Genesis 41: 25. Then Joseph said to Pharaoh, "The dreams of Pharaoh are one; God has shown Pharaoh what He is about to do:

God also gave king Nebuchadnezzar all the kingdoms of the earth and the beast of the field when he had not known God.

Jeremiah 27:5-8 'I have made the earth, the man and the beast that are on the ground, by My great power and by My outstretched arm, and have given it to whom it seemed proper to Me. And now I have given all these lands into the hand of Nebuchadnezzar the king of Babylon, My servant; and the beasts of the field I have also given him to serve him. So all nations shall serve him and his son and his son's son, until the time of his land comes; and then many nations and great kings shall make him serve them. And it shall be, that the nation and kingdom which will not serve Nebuchadnezzar the king of Babylon, and which will not put its neck under the yoke of the king of Babylon, that nation I will punish,' says the LORD, 'with the sword, the famine, and the pestilence, until I have consumed them by his hand.

The best an unbeliever would get from God can be likened to crumbs from the masters' table.

Matthew 15:27 And she said, "Yes, Lord, yet even the little dogs eat the crumbs which fall from their masters' table."

But there is a better way when we know him personally as Christians. God reserves the food on the table for His sons. The sons can have a buffet on the masters' table. Until, the heathen comes to the saving grace of the Lord, he does not enjoy the privilege of sonship.

<u>Kathryn Kuhlman's Account</u>: *Let's take the account of whom to pray to by Kathryn Kuhlman from the book, 'LORD TEACH US TO PRAY'.* [a]

It makes all the difference in the world to whom we pray. When Jesus prayed, He always addressed God as Father, and as our Heavenly Father, He will pity us is in our weaknesses and our infirmities. Neither the angels of heaven nor the saints who have gone into the presence of God have the power to answer prayer. They do not know our needs nor have the ability to supply our needs. Only one has that power and that is God Almighty, and we dishonor God when we pray to anyone else except God Almighty.

If you can look up and of a truth be able to say, MY HEAVENLY FATHER—if there is that glorious relationship between you and God, then you are one of the richest persons in the world. On the other hand, if you know God only as your creator, then you are one of the poorest persons living, despite the fact that you may possess great material wealth, you are bankrupt even though you may not be conscious of it if you cannot claim God as your Heavenly Father.

TWO

REASONS FOR PRAYERS

There are many reasons for prayers which include but not limited to the following:

- God commanded us to pray.

  Leviticus 6:12, 13 And the fire on the altar shall be kept burning on it; it shall not be put out. And the priest shall burn wood on it every morning, and lay the burnt offering in order on it; and he shall burn on it the fat of the peace offerings. A fire shall always be burning on the altar; it shall never go out.

- Christ made Himself as an example.

  Luke 5:16 So He Himself often withdrew into the wilderness and prayed.

- When we have time for the Lord, the Lord in turn will have time for us.

  Proverbs 8:17 I love those who love me, And those who seek me diligently will find me.

- Peace to reign.

  Psalm 122:6 Pray for the peace of Jerusalem: "May they prosper who love you.

Jeremiah 29:7 And seek the peace of the city where I have caused you to be carried away captive, and pray to the LORD for it; for in its peace you will have peace.

- He promised to answer us.

  Jeremiah 33:3 'Call to Me, and I will answer you, and show you great and mighty things, which you do not know.'

  Isaiah 65:24 "It shall come to pass That before they call, I will answer; And while they are still speaking, I will hear.

- To make our requests known to Him.

  Philippians 4:6 Be anxious for nothing, but in everything by prayer and supplication, with thanksgiving, let your requests be made known to God;

- It keeps us from evil and temptation.

  Luke 22:40 When He came to the place, He said to them, "Pray that you may not enter into temptation."

- Spiritual Fruit (Character): When we pray over a period of time, God's character (nature) begins to rob off on us as we allow Him.

  Galatians 5:22-23 But the fruit of the Spirit is love, joy, peace, longsuffering, kindness, goodness, faithfulness, gentleness, self-control. Against such there is no law.

- Spiritual Gifts (Anointing): When we pray over a period of time, God's anointing begins to increase in our lives. *1 Corinthians 12.*

- Lots more.

THREE

WHO CAN PRAY

Prayer is not restricted to the rich nor is it a compensation for the poor.

The learned does not have prayer as his exclusive right and cannot edge out the unlearned.

Prayer is also not gender sensitive. Men as well as women can pray.

Prayer is not restricted to regions. Everyone in every land can pray.

The new convert, nominal or established Christian can pray.

The sinner as well as the saint can pray.

Generally, it is not confined to age, sex, position, social status, cultures, education, race or religion. Everyone can pray. Nobody has a monopoly to prayer.

Every one can have access to God though the degree of access may differ.

Even people that are not Christians can pray and God does hear. Before most of us became Christians, God answered our prayers. Remember, asking God for salvation is a prayer we said while we were not yet saved and because we are now Christians does not mean God should not answer the prayers of those that are not Christians or are yet to be Christians.

An example is seen in the life of Cornelius, he was a devout man and one who feared God. God answered his prayers despite being a gentile at that time. God does some things in His sovereignty but He will never contradict His word—the Bible.

Acts 10:2 a devout man and one who feared God with all his household, who gave alms generously to the people, and prayed to God always.

It should be noted that the Christian has the best of both worlds as there are a lot of benefits when we have a relationship with God through the Lord Jesus Christ.

If you are reading this book and you do not have a relationship with God and you desire such relationship, you can simply close your eyes and say this prayer with all your heart.

> **LORD JESUS, I COME TO YOU TO SAVE MY SOUL TODAY. KINDLY, GO INTO MY PAST AND FORGIVE MY MULTITUDES OF SINS. CLEANSE ME BY YOUR BLOOD WHICH YOU SHED ON THE CROSS. COME AND WALK WITH ME PRESENTLY. SECURE MY FUTURE FOR YOUR GLORY. HELP ME TO FOLLOW YOU ALL THE WAY. I ACCEPT YOU TODAY AS MY PERSONAL LORD AND SAVIOUR. THANK YOU FOR ACCEPTING ME AS YOUR CHILD, IN JESUS NAME I PRAY. AMEN.**

Without reserving words, you are welcomed into the best group (Christianity) in the world. You are not welcomed into a religion but into a relationship with God. He is now your HEAVENLY FATHER. You have the Father of fathers as your father. It is an everyday walk. I would be glad to send you a booklet: LAYING A STRONG FOUNDATION IN CHRIST if you would like to develop deeper relationship with Him.

FOUR

LEARNING HOW TO PRAY

You learn to pray by praying not just talking about it. Develop the habit and pray from the HEART and not the HEAD. Some of the ways to learn HOW TO PRAY include:

- **Learning from the master—JESUS**: The best teacher when it comes to praying is Jesus Christ. Jesus remains the best in the business of prayer. When one has personal experience of Christ, gradually, one will begin to do what He does. The disciples asked Jesus to teach them how to pray. He taught them the Lord's Prayer. The Lord's Prayer is a model of prayer which is still relevant today.

Matthew 6: 9-13

Our Father, who art in heaven,
Hallowed be thy Name.
Thy kingdom come.
Thy will be done,
On earth as it is in heaven.
Give us this day our daily bread.
And forgive us our trespasses,
As we forgive those who trespass against us.
And lead us not into temptation,
But deliver us from evil.
For thine is the kingdom,
and the power,
and the glory,
for ever and ever.
Amen.

- **The Holy Spirit**: Many people pray general prayers while not addressing the main source of the issue. The Holy Spirit helps us to pray aright because He knows the mind of the Father about specific situations.

  John 16:12-13 "I still have many things to say to you, but you cannot bear them now. However, when He, the Spirit of truth, has come, He will guide you into all truth; for He will not speak on His own authority, but whatever He hears He will speak; and He will tell you things to come.

  Romans 8:26 Likewise the Spirit also helps in our weaknesses. For we do not know what we should pray for as we ought, but the Spirit Himself makes intercession for us with groaning which cannot be uttered.

- **Having a Desire/Passion**: Whatever someone has a passion or desire for, he or she does. Apply your heart to prayer.

  Genesis 11:6 And the LORD said, Indeed the people are one, and they have all one language; and this they begin to do and now <u>nothing they have proposed to do will be withheld from them.</u>

- **The place of Mentors and Coaches**: To be successful in business, you need people in business that are ahead of you. To be successful in football, having a coach is a good decision. To be successful in politics, you need an established politician. To be successful in your career, you might need someone who is ahead of you in that field. Prayer is not an exception—you might just need a prayer mentor.

  Proverbs 13:20 He who walks with wise men will be wise. But the companion of fools will be destroyed.

- **Take Baby Steps**: Babes do not start with heavy solid food but with little quantity of milk. Most great things start small. Start praying for one minute daily and make it consistent. If you pray daily for 21 days, it becomes part of you. When you have gained mastery of one minute of daily prayer, you can leap to two minutes, five minutes and so on.

Job 8:7 Though your <u>beginning was small</u>, Yet your latter end would increase abundantly.

- **Close the Eyes**: While growing up in the Christian faith, perhaps at Sunday school level, we were told to close our eyes in order not to be distracted. However, as one progresses and the heart is tuned, you may not close the eyes every time especially when engaged in activities like cooking or driving.

- **Prayer Cells**: Two are better than one (*Ecclesiastes 4:9a*). Prayer cells not only help you in knowing how to pray but also keep you accountable.

Proverbs 27:17 Iron sharpens iron, So a man sharpens the countenance of his friend.

- **Schedules**: Some people have specific schedules for prayers which they follow regularly. Others will only pray when they come to their wits end and are left with no alternative than to pray. It is more profitable to be schedule—driven as Jesus expects us to pray without ceasing. It is also helpful to know yourself and what works for you.

Ecclesiastes 3:1 To everything there is a season, A Time for every purpose under heaven.

- **Books**: Invest in books, tapes, electronic books and other materials that deal with prayer.

Daniel 9:2 in the first year of his reign I, Daniel, <u>understood by books</u> the number of years specified by the word of the LORD through Jeremiah the prophet, that he would accomplish seventy years in the desolation of Jerusalem.

- **Prayer Lists**: You can easily get bored as a starter or distracted or become short of words. A list helps you focus and get you going.

- **Prayer Meetings, Conferences, Seminars and Vigils:** The Bible admonished us not to forsake the assembling of ourselves together (*Hebrews 10:25*). Corporate prayers at conferences, vigils and seminars go a long way in developing our prayer life.

- **Lots more.**

<u>Note</u>: In order to pray effectively in the open, you must learn to settle things in your closet before manifestation in the open. If you pray regularly in your closet, praying in the open will not be a big task and as time goes on, the reward is certain.

Matthew 6:6 But you, when you pray, go into your room, and when you have shut your door, pray to your Father who is in the secret place; and your Father who sees in secret will reward you openly

HOW NOT TO PRAY

There are also ways NOT to pray which include but not limited to:

- **Being Hypocritical**

Matthew 6:5 "And when you pray, you shall not be like the hypocrites. For they love to pray standing in the synagogues and on the corners of the streets, that they may be seen by men. Assuredly, I say to you, they have their reward

- **Using Vain Repetitions**

Matthew 6:7 And when you pray, do not use vain repetitions as the heathen do. For they think that they will be heard for their many words.

- **Lots more.**

FIVE

BENEFITS OF PRAYER

(ADVANTAGES)

There are many advantages of prayers which include but not limited to the following:

- Power.

  James 5:16b The effective fervent prayer of the righteous man avails much.

- Provision.

  Philippians 4:19 And my God shall supply all your need according to His riches in glory by Christ Jesus.

- Protection.

  Psalm 91: 1-end.

- Direction.

  Psalm 32:8 I will instruct you and teach you the way you should go; I will guide you with My eye.

- Develops deeper relationship with God.

  John 15:4-5 Abide in Me, and I in you. As the branch cannot bear fruit of itself, unless it abides in the vine, neither can you, unless you abide in Me. "I am the vine, you are the branches. He who abides in Me, and I in him, bears much fruit; for without Me you can do nothing.

- Deliverance.
  2 Corinthians 1:10 who delivered us from so great a death, and does deliver us; in whom we trust that He will still deliver us,

- Miracles.

  Jeremiah 33:3 Call to Me, and I will answer you, and show you great and mighty things, which you do not know.'

- Wisdom, Knowledge and an Understanding Heart, *James 1:5, Daniel 1:17*

  1 Kings 3:12 behold, I have done according to your words; see, I have given you a wise and understanding heart, so that there has not been anyone like you before you, nor shall any like you arise after you.

- Subdue the Adversary *2 Chronicles 20:16-25.*

- Forgiveness and Healing of the land.

  2 Chronicles 7:14 if My people who are called by My name will humble themselves, and pray and seek My face, and turn from their wicked ways, then I will hear from heaven, and will forgive their sin and heal their land.

- Confidence.

  1 John 5:14 Now this is the confidence that we have in Him, that if we ask anything according to His will, He hears us.

- Avert calamities/Destruction.

  Jonah 3:10 Then God saw their works, that they turned from their evil way; and God relented from the disaster that He had said He would bring upon them, and He did not do it.

- Open Doors.

  Revelation 3:8 "I know your works. See, I have set before you an open door, and no one can shut it; for you have a little strength, have kept My word, and have not denied My name.

- God's Presence/Glory. *Exodus 33:13-14.*

  2 Chronicles 7:1 when Solomon had finished praying, fire came down from heaven and consumed the burnt offering and the sacrifices; and the glory of the LORD filled the temple.

- Strength.

  Philippians 4:13 I have strength for all things in Christ Who empowers me [I am ready for anything and equal to anything through Him Who infuses inner strength into me; I am self-sufficient in Christ's sufficiency].—Amplified Bible.

- Healing.

  James 5:16 Confess your trespasses to one another, and pray for one another, that you may be healed. The effective, fervent prayer of a righteous man avails much.

- Right Workers, Dependable Associates, Partners for Harvest.

  Matthew 9:38 Therefore pray the Lord of the harvest to send out laborers into His harvest."

- Angelic Assistance.

  2 Kings 19:35 And it came to pass on a certain night that the angel of the LORD went out, and killed in the camp of the Assyrians one hundred and eighty-five thousand; and when people arose early in the morning, there were the corpses—all dead.

- Increase in Confidence, Assurance, Faith and Boldness.

  Acts 4:31 And when they had prayed, the place where they were assembled together was shaken; and they were all filled with the Holy Spirit, and they spoke the word of God with boldness.

- Lots more.

SIX

PRAYER TIMES

We can pray at anytime of the day. As we consistently spend time with the Lord, our prayer time becomes more of a communion. It is a good practice to have a specific time or a specific place for prayer as it helps to develop a prayer culture. Early morning is often regarded as the best time for communion or conversation with the LORD while midnight is often regarded as the best times for warfare or deliverance prayers. Examples of the time of the day to pray include:

- <u>Early Morning</u>: It is often regarded as the best time to secure the day. When one rises early to commune and command the day with God on a consistent basis, God goes ahead of you and takes care of the events of the rest of the day. Many great saints of old rose up early to pray.

  Mark 1:35 Now in the morning, having risen a long while before daylight, He went out and departed to a solitary place; and there He prayed.

  Job 38:12-13 "Have you commanded the morning since your days began, And caused the dawn to know its place, That it might take hold of the ends of the earth, And the wicked be shaken out of it?

- <u>Afternoon</u>: Many are so pre-occupied with the business of the day that prayer is neglected completely at such a time. However, wise business men and women take their time off for mid-day prayers.
  *Acts 10:9 The next day, as they went on their journey and drew near the city, Peter went up on the housetop to pray, about the sixth hour. (**12 noon**)*

*Acts 10:3 About the ninth hour (**3 pm or 1500 hours**) of the day he saw clearly in a vision an angel of God coming in and saying to him, "Cornelius!"*

- Evening: It is good to wind up the day with prayer. You can say one or two words before going to bed at night.

1 Kings 18:36-38 And it came to pass, at the time of the offering of the evening sacrifice, that Elijah the prophet came near and said, "LORD God of Abraham, Isaac, and Israel, let it be known this day that You are God in Israel and I am Your servant, and that I have done all these things at Your word. Hear me, O LORD, hear me, that this people may know that You are the LORD God, and that You have turned their hearts back to You again."

Then the fire of the LORD fell and consumed the burnt sacrifice, and the wood and the stones and the dust, and it licked up the water that was in the trench.

- Midnight: This is often regarded as the best time for warfare and deliverance prayers. It is also a time to pull resources from heaven. It is in the night that evil seeds are sown in the lives of men (*Matthew 13: 25*). Spiritual battles are fought and won at night.

Acts 16:25 But at midnight Paul and Silas were praying and singing hymns to God, and the prisoners were listening to them.

Luke 21:37 And in the daytime He was teaching in the temple, but at night He went out and stayed on the mountain called Olivet.

In order to pray without ceasing, it is not a bad idea if we have a specific time that we converse with God (early morning, afternoon, evening and mid night—select the moment that is best suited for you).

In addition to the specific time, one can be praying consciously or unconsciously in his heart throughout the rest of the day. This practice keeps you in touch with the throne of grace and makes you spiritually sensitive. You can pick up spiritual signals easily.

SEVEN

PRAYER HINDRANCES

Some of the hindrances to prayers include:

A. Sin

Isaiah 59:1-2 Behold, the LORD's hand is not shortened, That it cannot save;

Nor His ear heavy, That it cannot hear. But your iniquities have separated you from your God; and your sins have hidden His face from you, So that He will not hear

Galatians 5:19-21 Now the works of the flesh are evident, which are: adultery, fornication, uncleanness, lewdness, idolatry, sorcery, hatred, contentions, jealousies, outbursts of wrath, selfish ambitions, dissensions, heresies, envy, murders, drunkenness, revelries, and the like; of which I tell you beforehand, just as I also told you in time past, that those who practice such things will not inherit the kingdom of God.

Psalm 66:18 If I regard iniquity in my heart, The Lord will not hear.

- Unforgiveness
- Immorality
- Unrighteousness
- Drunkenness
- Anger
- Jealousy
- Malice

- Covetousness
- Idolatry
- Envy
- Murder
- Pride
- Hatred
- Selfish ambitions
- Sorcery
- Mention the one that is common with you if not already mentioned above!
- Lots more

B. Laziness *Proverbs 6:9-10*

C. Busyness *1 Kings 20:40*

D. Indifference: *Proverbs 6:9-10*

E. Procrastination *Proverbs 24:33-34*

F. Sleep or fatigue: *Luke 22:45,*

G. Clouded mind, Wandering minds

H. Self Righteousness/Self Justification *Luke 18:10-14.*

I. Disagreement in a group *Amos 3:3*

J. Double mindedness. *James 1:6, Ecclesiastes 9:10*

K. Asking amiss *James 4:3,*

L. Lots more.

EIGHT

PRAYER INTENSITY

(TEMPERAMENT)

A. INTRODUCTION TO TEMPERAMENT

Tim LaHaye's Account*: Let's take an account of temperament by __Tim LaHaye__ from his book 'THE SPIRIT CONTROLLED TEMPERAMENT'.[a]*

There is nothing more fascinating about people than their inherited temperament! It is temperament that provides each human being with the distinguishing qualities that make each as individually unique as the differing designs God has given to snowflakes. Temperament is the unseen force underlying human action, a force that can destroy a normal and productive human being unless it is disciplined and directed.

Temperament provides both our strengths and weaknesses. Although we like to think only of our strengths, everyone has weaknesses!

God has given Christians the Holy Spirit, who is able to improve our natural strengths and overcome our weaknesses as we cooperate with him.

Temperament is the combination of inborn traits that subconsciously affects all our behavior. These traits, which are passed on by our genes, are based on hereditary factors and arranged at the time of conception. Six people contribute through the gene pool to the makeup of every baby: two parents and four grandparents. Some authorities suggest that we may get more genes from our grandparents than our parents. That could account for the greater resemblance of some children to their grandparents than to their parents. The alignment of temperament traits, though unseen, is just as predictable as the colour of eyes, hair, or size of body.

It is a person's temperament that makes that person outgoing and extrovertish or shy and introvertish. Doubtless you know both kinds of people who are siblings—born to the same parents. Similarly, it is temperament that makes some people art or music enthusiasts, while others are sports or industry minded.

The four temperaments are:

1. Sanguine

The Sanguine temperament personality is fairly extroverted. People of a sanguine temperament tend to enjoy social gatherings, making new friends and tend to be quite loud. They are usually quite creative and often daydream. However, some alone time is crucial for those of this temperament. Sanguine can also be very sensitive, compassionate and thoughtful. Sanguine personalities generally struggle with following tasks all the way through, are chronically late, and tend to be forgetful and sometimes a little sarcastic. Often, when pursuing a new hobby, interest is lost quickly when it ceases to be engaging or fun. They are very much people persons. They are talkative and not shy. For some people, these are the ones you want to be friends with and usually they become life long friends.

2. Choleric

A person who is choleric is a do-er. They have a lot of ambition, energy, and passion, and try to instill it in others. They can dominate people of other temperaments, especially phlegmatic types. Many great charismatic military and political figures were cholerics. They like to be leaders and in charge of everything.

3. Melancholic

A person who is a thoughtful ponderer has a *melancholic* disposition. Often very considerate and get rather worried when they could not be on time for. Melancholics can be highly creative in activities such as poetry and art; they can become preoccupied with the tragedy and cruelty in the world. A *melancholic* is also a perfectionist. They are often self-reliant and independent; one negative part of being a melancholic is that sometimes they can get so involved in what they are doing they forget to think of others.

4. Phlegmatic

Phlegmatics tend to be self-content and kind. They can be very accepting and affectionate. They may be very receptive and shy and often prefer stability to uncertainty and change. They are very consistent, relaxed, rational, curious, and observant, making them good administrators. However they can also be very passive aggressive.

Note: Some people have combinations of these temperaments.

B. EFFECT OF TEMPERAMENTS ON PRAYER

The tone or degree in prayer depends on the temperament (4 temperaments) of the person praying. Some people just have their lips moving (Hannah in *1 Samuel 1:13*), some have it very audible, otherwise *John 17* would not have been recorded, some groan, some normal conversation and many more. All is permissible as long as you are not impressing anyone.

Prayer nature of the four Temperaments:

1. Sanguine:

They are a bit loud when it comes to prayers. They can be praying and get engaged in other activities conveniently. They would have finished praying before considering what the prayer point is about. If they make mistakes, they will run straight into prayers.

2. Choleric:

They are very loud and mostly aggressive when they pray. They want to always get the best of result and do not easily take NO for an answer. They pray with authority and feel they are best suited to lead prayers in a group while every other member of the group takes instructions. They can handle all kinds of prayers and most people of this personality have the calling of an apostle.

3. Phlegmatic:

They cannot be said to be loud and cannot be said to be quiet when it comes to praying. They accept whatever form (outcome) the prayer takes.

4. Melancholic:

They are very quiet when they pray. They look at all sides (natural and supernatural) before jumping into prayers. They are very thoughtful and make meditation a great part of their prayers. They will not argue with you when you raise 'funny prayer requests' around them but they have a mind or spirit of their own to search things out in order to find out the truth. They are mostly counselors. They feel terrible about themselves should they make mistakes, and reluctantly head back into prayers.

NINE

PRAYER LISTS AND RECORDS

A record is a collection of accounts or events for information.

A list is a collection of connected items. You can make a prayer list for mission outreach, wedding ceremony, each member of the family, business, etc.

Importance of prayer list: A prayer list is a number of linked requests broken down into items. The following underscores the importance of prayer lists:

- It serves as a guide as to how to pray
- It helps to maintain focus
- It helps to persevere in prayers
- It gives an analysis
- Lots more.

R. Kent Hughes's Account: *Let's take an account of a prayer list by R. Kent Hughes from his book DISCIPLINES OF A GODLY MAN. Chapter seven of the book talks about discipline of prayers*[4]

Quite frankly, I could not get on at all without a prayer list, not only because it tames my wondering mind, but also because it insures that I will not neglect things that are important to me, including the many requests for personal prayer which I receive. Without a prayer list, my promises to "pray for you" would be totally empty. In addition, a prayer list is perfect for keeping track of answers to prayers.

Prayer Records: The Bible is a record. A prayer record is a past account kept for information purposes. The following underscores the importance of prayer records:

- It helps in reflecting the past and hence dependence on and appreciating God
- It helps in projection into the future
- It helps in evaluating the present
- It helps to avoid mistakes from the present and past.
- Lots more.

Note: Do not keep records of those that hurt you, release such to God and let go in your mind. As you release them in your mind, God will settle you in due time.

TEN

PRAYER GROUPS AND AGREEMENTS

The importance of having a prayer cell, prayer group, prayer chain, prayer team or prayer network cannot be overemphasized. Some scriptures that support such include:

> *Ecclesiastes 4:9 Two are better than one, because they have a good reward for their labor.*

> *Deuteronomy 32:30 How could one chase a thousand and two will put ten thousand to flight, unless their Rock had sold them, And the LORD had surrendered them?*

Some Biblical examples include:

• **Daniel and His Team:**

There was a team of four boys brought to Babylon from Jerusalem. They were far from home but they did not lose focus of where they came from and what they needed to do to keep fit and adapt in the land they found themselves. Although, they settled down very well in the foreign land, they did not allow the king's food and other distractions make them lose track of home. They were a balanced set of boys. They could not prevent themselves being carried away to Babylon but they made the best use of the situation. While other exiles were crying by the rivers of Babylon, these four looked at the situation from a different perspective and formed a prayer team. In addition to forming a prayer team, they formed a tutorial group in school. When Daniel was promoted to the position of vice president, he recommended his friends and they got to the top in the country's administration.

Daniel 1:17, 20 As for these four young men, God gave them knowledge and skill in all literature and wisdom; and Daniel had understanding in all visions and dreams. And in all matters of wisdom and understanding about which the king examined them, he found them ten times better than all the magicians and astrologers who were in all his realm.

Daniel 2:17-19 Then Daniel went to his house, and made the decision known to Hananiah, Mishael, and Azariah, his companions, that they might seek mercies from the God of heaven concerning this secret, so that Daniel and his companions might not perish with the rest of the wise men of Babylon. Then the secret was revealed to Daniel in a night vision. So Daniel blessed the God of heaven.

Daniel 2:48-49 Then the king promoted Daniel and gave him many great gifts; and he made him ruler over the whole province of Babylon, and chief administrator over all the wise men of Babylon. Also Daniel petitioned the king, and he set Shadrach, Meshach, and Abed-Nego over the affairs of the province of Babylon; but Daniel sat in the gate of the king.

- **The Apostles**: When the apostles were threatened, they went to their own companions and prayed.

Acts 4:23-24 And being let go, they went to their own companions and reported all that the chief priests and elders had said to them. So when they heard that, they raised their voice to God with one accord and said: "Lord, You are God, who made heaven and earth and the sea, and all that is in them,

- **Moses, Aaron and Hur**: When Israel was fighting with Amalek, Moses would not have made it alone with the rod of God in his hands without the support of Aaron and Hur.

Exodus 17:10-13 So Joshua did as Moses said to him, and fought with Amalek. And Moses, Aaron, and Hur went up to the top of the hill. And so it was, when Moses held up his hand, that Israel prevailed; and when he let down his hand, Amalek prevailed. But Moses' hands became heavy; so they took a stone and put it under him, and he sat on it. And Aaron and Hur supported his hands, one on one side, and the other on the other side; and his hands were steady until the going down of the sun. So Joshua defeated Amalek and his people with the edge of the sword.

- **Israel in a foreign land**: Esther requested for prayer so as to spare the whole nation in exile from execution.

  Esther 4:15-16 Then Esther told them to reply to Mordecai: "Go, gather all the Jews who are present in Shushan, and fast for me; neither eat nor drink for three days, night or day. My maids and I will fast likewise. And so I will go to the king, which is against the law; and if I perish, I perish!"

- **Lots more.**

PUTTING IT INTO PRACTICE

<u>Pastoral Network</u>: In this information age, it is not a bad idea for there to be a network of Christians (ministers) from different regions (states, countries and even continents) forming prayer chains and exchanging ideas and other information.

<u>Politics</u>: Most military men that ruled in Nigeria met and became friends while at the military school.

Some politicians also met one way or the other in the past either while at higher institutions or during their national service year. When Daniel was promoted as ruler in the whole province of Babylon, he recommended his friends to the king. No wonder Daniel still had time to pray despite his busy schedules. Most likely he had his men that could be of assistance to him one way or the other and the kings business did not suffer.

<u>Footballers:</u> The more footballers play together, the more they tend to blend together. Some footballers that have played at the junior level have ended up playing together at the senior level. Birds of a feather flock together. Prayer should not be an exception.

<u>Study Groups</u>: I recall while in school, we had a tutorial group. This group had all the past questions from about five previous sets, all recommended reading materials by our lecturers, complete lecture notes as well as solutions to all tests and assignments given in class. I remember sometimes after studying together at night, they often requested that I be the one that round up with prayers. We all excelled and were amongst the best in class. Most of us are still in touch with one another today.

Caution: There must always be agreements within groups to strengthen their prayers and ensure lasting results.

Amos 3:3 Can two walk together, unless they are agreed?

As taught by our Lord Christ, prayer and agreement in a group are inseparable

Matthew 18:19-20 "Again I say to you that if two of you <u>agree</u> on earth concerning anything that they <u>ask</u>, it will be done for them by My Father in heaven. For where two or three are gathered together in My name, I am there in the midst of them."

The place of agreement cannot be over emphasized as evident in the building of the tower of Babel. The tower started and got to an advanced stage because the people had one mind to work together and nothing could stop them. Unfortunately, they left God and prayer out of the equation. The project eventually became an exercise in futility.

Genesis 11:6 And the LORD said, Indeed the people are one, and they have all one language; and this they begin to do and now nothing they have proposed to do will be withheld from them.

Genesis 11:7-8 Come, let Us go down and there confuse their language, that they may not understand one another's speech." So the LORD scattered them abroad from there over the face of all the earth, and they ceased building the city.

In contract, the walls of Jerusalem were built successfully because the people had a mind to work together despite opposition. They involved God and prayed. The project was speedily executed.

Nehemiah 4:6 So we built the wall, and the entire wall was joined together up to half its height: for the people had a mind to work.

Nehemiah 4:9 Nevertheless we made our prayer to our God and because of them, we set a watch against them day and night.

It is better to address the issue of agreement in a group before praying together. When you want to choose a life partner, business partner, close aids, and other decisions with far reaching effects, ensure you are in agreement before forging ahead with prayers.

Related Experience: I went visiting a young couple whose marriage was under two months old. I decided to pray when leaving but the husband was reluctant about joining us in prayers. I could read between the lines that the couples were not in agreement and the union was soon headed for the rocks, so we looked at the issues from all sides and they both forgave each other and came into agreement. Then we prayed. I mean we prayed. I had testimonies about their love life some days after.

Be careful and watchful of people that come into your team or circle of influence as not everyone has the same set of objectives. There are some people with sinister moves. With prayer and gift of discernment, you can fish out those with ulterior motives and get them flushed out before they sink everyone in the team like the case of Jonah in the ship. There was no peace until Jonah was thrown out. As stated earlier, only birds of a feather should flock together.

Proverbs 25:4-5 Take away the dross from silver and it will go to the silversmith for jewelry. Take away the wicked before the king and his throne will be established in righteousness

ELEVEN

PRAYER PLACES
(VENUES)

You can pray anywhere and **everywhere** but not any how—God is omni present and there is no distance in the realm of the spirit. It is not a bad idea if we have a specific place to pray but get to know what works best for you and stick to it. When you consistently pray and find favour with Him, GOD can be as near as your breath.

1 Timothy 2:8 I desire therefore that the men pray **everywhere***, lifting up holy hands, without wrath and doubting.*

Some of the places to pray include but not limited to the following:

- **Your House**: Bed Room, Sitting Room, Kitchen, Dinning Table, Bath Room, Garage or anywhere in the house even the Toilet!.

   Act 9:11 And the Lord said unto him, Arise, and go into the street which is called Straight, and inquire in the house of Judas for one called Saul of Tarsus: for, behold, he is praying

- **When in transit:** In the Car, Bus, Plane, Ship, Space Shuttle or while walking but open your eyes if you are driving. Jonah was on a ship sailing to Tarshish and the sailors prayed. Paul was on a ship going to Rome (they fasted aboard for 14 days as recorded in Acts 27)

Jonah 1:14 Therefore they cried out to the LORD and said, "We pray, O LORD, please do not let us perish for this man's life, and do not charge us with innocent blood; for You, O LORD, have done as it pleased You."

- **Mountains, Fields, Gardens or Wilderness:** Some prayers might require separation.

Exodus 19:20 And the LORD came down upon mount Sinai, on the top of the mount and the LORD called Moses up to the top of the mount; and Moses went up.

Mark 9:2 And after six days Jesus took with him Peter, and James, and John, and led them up on a high mountain apart by themselves: and He was transfigured before them.

Luke 5:16 So He Himself often withdrew into the wilderness and prayed.

- **Place of Worship**—Church, Crusade grounds, Temple.

2 Chronicles 7:1 when Solomon had finished praying, fire came down from heaven and consumed the burnt offering and the sacrifices; and the glory of the LORD filled the temple

2 Kings 19:14-15 And Hezekiah received the letter from the hand of the messengers, and read it; and Hezekiah went up to the house of the LORD, and spread it before the LORD. Then Hezekiah prayed before the LORD, and said: "O LORD God of Israel, the One who dwells between the cherubim, You are God, You alone, of all the kingdoms of the earth. You have made heaven and earth.

Matthew 21:13 And He said to them, "It is written, 'My house shall be called a house of prayer but you have made it a 'den of thieves.

- **Prison**—Paul & Silas.

Act 16:24-25 having received such a charge, he put them into the inner prison, and fastened their feet in the stocks. And at midnight Paul and Silas were praying, and singing hymns to God: and the prisoners were listening to them.

- **Dangerous Environments.** There are some environments one never planned to be but for reasons beyond one's control.

  <u>Examples:</u> Jonah in the belly of the fish and Daniel in the Den of Lions (*Daniel 6:16-22*). Some people have found themselves in slaughter houses and God miraculously intervened.

  Jonah 2:1 Then Jonah prayed to the LORD his God from the fish's belly.

- **Lots more.**

TWELVE

PRAYER POSTURES (POSITIONS)

It makes little or no difference the position adopted when praying. All postures are right as long as the heart is tuned and there is communication with GOD. Note the posture(s) that suits you.

- **Kneel**

  Luke 22:41 He withdrew about a stone's throw beyond them, <u>knelt down</u> and prayed

  Daniel 6:10 Now when Daniel knew that the writing was signed, he went home. And in his upper room, with his windows open toward Jerusalem, <u>he knelt down on his knees</u> three times that day, and prayed and gave thanks before his God, as was his custom since early days.

- **Prostrate, lay flat, roll on the floor**

  Joshua 7:6 Then Joshua tore his clothes, and <u>fell to the earth on his face</u> before the ark of the LORD until evening, he and the elders of Israel; and they put dust on their heads.

  Job 1:20 Then Job arose, tore his robe, and shaved his head; and he <u>fell to the ground</u> and worshiped.

  Deuteronomy 9:25 "Thus I <u>prostrated myself</u> before the LORD; forty days and forty nights I kept prostrating myself, because the LORD had said He would destroy you.

- **Stand to pray, Bow down, face between knees**

  Genesis 18:22 Then the men turned away from there and went toward Sodom, but Abraham still <u>stood</u> before the LORD.

  1 Kings 18:42-44 So Ahab went up to eat and drink. And Elijah went up to the top of Carmel: then he bowed down on the ground, and <u>put his face between his knees</u>, and said to his servant, "Go up now, look towards the sea "So he went up and looked, and said "there is nothing" And seven times he said, "Go again" Then it came to pass the seventh time, that he said, there is a cloud as small as a man's hand, rising out of the sea! So he said, "Go up say to Ahab, Prepare your chariot, and go down before the rain stops you"

- **Walking, Pacing, Marching**

  Joshua 6:3 You shall <u>march around</u> the city, all you men of war, you shall go round the city once. This you shall do in six days.

- **Lifting up your hands**

  1 Timothy 2:8 I desire therefore that the men pray everywhere, <u>lifting up</u> holy hands, without wrath and doubting.

- **Sitting down, crawling**

  Exodus 17: 12 But Moses' hands became heavy; so they took a stone and put it under him, and he <u>sat</u> on it. And Aaron and Hur supported his hands, one on one side, and the other on the other side; and his hands were steady until the going down of the sun.

- **Lots more.**

THIRTEEN

PRAYER RESPONSES

(ANSWERS)

As long as our prayers get to God, He always answers. He does not keep a secretary or deputy to turn us away.

Jeremiah 33:3 Call to Me, and I will answer you, and show you great and mighty things, which you do not know.'

However, answers from GOD could be one of the following:

YES
NO
WAIT

1. **YES Example:** God, I want to know you more. I want to increase in righteousness. I want all that pertains to life and godliness. As long as we pray inline with God's will, the answer will always be a YES (God's answer will also always be a YES as long as you can handle it).

   Matthew 7:11If you then, being evil, know how to give good gifts to your children, how much more will your Father who is in heaven give good things to those who ask Him!

   Numbers 23:19 God is not a man, that He should lie, Nor a son of man, that He should repent. Has He said, and will He not do? Or has He spoken, and will He not make it good?

1 Thessalonians 5:24 He who calls you is faithful, who also will do it.

But if you insist on contrary things, God may allow you to have your way but it may eventually destroy you.

Psalm 106:15 And He gave them their request; but sent leanness into their soul.

Note: Sometimes when the answer is a YES, there could be a delay in getting its manifestation (*Daniel 9:12-13*) or the answer could even be beyond what we requested for (*Ephesians 3:20*)

2. **NO Example**: A student that prays against taking examinations is only kidding himself or herself. God's response will be to prepare for the examination. Jesus was to face the CROSS and He was praying that the cross should go away. GOD Almighty didn't change His mind but gave Him the strength to face the cross. God gives you strength to go through some things that are necessary.

    Isaiah 43:2 When you pass through the waters, I will be with you; and through the rivers they shall not overflow you: when thou walk through the fire, you shall not be burned; nor shall the flame scorch you.

    2 Corinthians 12:8-9 Concerning this thing I pleaded with the Lord three times that it might depart from me. And He said to me, "My grace is sufficient for you, for My strength is made perfect in weakness." Therefore most gladly I will rather boast in my infirmities, that the power of Christ may rest upon me.

    Sometimes we ask wrongly

    James 4:3 You ask and do not receive, because you ask amiss, that you may spend it on your pleasures.

    After a period of time, when we have gained wisdom and understanding or we are matured, we would be grateful that God's responses to some of our prayers were not initially granted.

3. **WAIT Example:** If an underage says he or she wants to get married, God will say wait. God does not give us what we can not handle because of His love for us but allows us to mature or go through due processes before giving us some things.

Habakkuk 2:3 For the vision is yet for an appointed time; But at the end it will speak, and it will not lie. Though it tarries, wait for it; Because it will surely come, It will not tarry

However, when we insist on our way, we most times have our way but it will not be God's best for us. We must seek the GOOD, ACCEPTABLE AND PERFECT will of God.

Romans 12:2 And do not be conformed to this world, but be transformed by the renewing of your mind, that you may prove what is that good and acceptable and perfect will of God.

God wants to give us the best (PERFECT WILL OF GOD) in all areas of our lives, most of the perfect will take time and also there might be a need to go through some processes and preparation. However, when we can not wait or we are very much in a hurry, God will reluctantly give its permissive (ACCEPTABLE OR GOOD) will.

And the worst case happens when we leave God out of the equation, it results in BAD will. An example can be seen from prophet Balaam's prayer after knowing God's will as recorded in *Numbers 22-24.*

Note: Regardless of what the answer from God might be (yes, no, or wait) to any situation we may face now or in future, His thoughts for us are thoughts of peace and not of evil. As long as we remain in the centre of His will, we will always have God's best for our lives.

Jeremiah 29:11 For I know the thoughts that I think toward you, says the LORD, thoughts of peace and not of evil, to give you a future and a hope.

FOURTEEN

PRAYER MAINTENANCE

Here we examine prayers from a maintenance point of view and we give analogy using the tyres of a car. We look at three prayer maintenance cultures namely: PREVENTIVE PRAYERS, PREDICTIVE PRAYERS AND CORRECTIVE PRAYERS.

1. **Preventive Prayers**: These are prayers offered to avoid, stop, foil, thwart or nip a pending problem in the bud. Prayers are offered to arrest issues before the problems become obvious. Preventive prayers help to develop a good detection mechanism before danger is fully blown. A little regular prayer in advance is worth more than a long prayer in arrears. Or better put, you pray so that you would not be a prey. Most people that lead consistent successful lives thrive on preventive prayers. They always have enough resources in their prayer bank which they withdraw at will and they often walk in fruitfulness, multiplication and dominion.

   Proverbs 22:3 A prudent man foresees evil and hides himself, But the simple pass on and are punished.

Biblical Example:

   DANIEL—It is strongly believed that it was not the prayer that Daniel prayed in the lion's den that prevented lions from making a dinner of him. It is certain that he prayed regularly BEFORE being thrown there (*Daniel 6:10*). This was the reason he enjoyed angelic presence in the lion's den (*Daniel 6:22*).

<u>Car Analogy</u>: For someone driving a car, the driver would be careful on the road should he come across sharp objects; he would slow down and take another path in order to avoid damage to the tyres of his car. This also saves him time repairing his tyres.

2. **Predictive Prayers**: There are some situations that you can not shy away from. We just have to brace up and face them squarely. These are also prayers that strengthen us for tough situations. You pray until your prayer bank is filled with enough resources that you can withdraw from in times of need.

Isaiah 43:2 When you pass through the waters, I will be with you; And through the rivers, they shall not overflow you. When you walk through the fire, you shall not be burned, Nor shall the flame scorch you.

Biblical Example:

JESUS—When Jesus was to face the cross and after much battle with the flesh, He surrendered His will to the Father. After praying in the garden, He was strengthened to face the cross. He would not have been able to face the cross without that prayer in the garden.

Luke 22:40-43 When He came to the place, He said to them, "Pray that you may not enter into temptation." And He was withdrawn from them about a stone's throw, and He knelt down and prayed, saying, "Father, if it is Your will, take this cup away from Me; nevertheless not My will, but Yours, be done." Then an angel appeared to Him from heaven, strengthening Him.

Five wise virgins took extra oil in their lamps

<u>Car Analogy</u>: No matter how careful we are, a flat tyre is sometimes inevitable. It is a wise idea to carry an extra tyre. Predictive prayers foresee such, so that when we come across the inevitable hiccups in life, we are strengthened to move on.

3. **Corrective Prayers**: These are prayers of repentance, redemption, deliverance, forgiveness or atonement. When some one makes

a mistake; he needs to get back to God. Sometimes we are not involved directly in the mistake (parents' sins, nation's sins, leadership's blunder, and so on). Corrective prayers are needed. To obey is better than sacrifice (*1 Samuel 15:22*). Either there are no resources in the prayer bank or the resources present have been abused or depleted. A bail out plan from heaven is needed as soon as possible. As much as possible walk in obedience and reduce corrective prayers to the barest minimum. If we are disciplined and obedient, there would be no need for certain prayers; to be candid—if we are disciplined, we can avoid the need for some deliverance prayers.

Proverbs 28:13 He who covers his sins will not prosper, But whoever confesses and forsakes them will have mercy.

1 John 1:8-9 If we say that we have no sin, we deceive ourselves, and the truth is not in us. If we confess our sins, He is faithful and just to forgive us our sins and to cleanse us from all unrighteousness.

Biblical Examples:

JONAH—*Jonah 1:19* Jonah had no business being in the belly of the fish but for his disobedience to an earlier instruction from God. Likewise, most of us have no business in some situations we get ourselves into. We should be thankful because God is not just wonderful and faithful but He is MERCIFUL. When we cry to Him in any situation we find ourselves, His mercy will locate and bring us out. You can not face the rest of the situation alone since you can not afford to sink further! May His mercy deliver us from ugly situations we walked into! Amen.

DAVID—*2 Samuel 11* David did not fall into immorality in a day but he walked into it gradually with the series of wrong steps he took over a period of time. If he had gone to battle inline with his duty as a king, he would not have been on the roof top. If he had not been on the roof top, he would not have seen what he should not see. If he had walked away from the roof top, he would not have had the final blow. He would not have had to also pray and fast for seven days afterwards. However, he repented and his corrective prayer is recorded in *Psalm 32 and 51.*

<u>Car Analogy</u>: If we carelessly run the tyre of our car on sharp objects, the tyre would be punctured. Thus, the tyre would need to be vulcanised or replaced. The repair and replacement takes time and it also involves cost and effort.

FIFTEEN

BALANCING PRAYER AND WORK

We want to examine what prayer can do and what prayer is not expected to do. There needs to be equilibrium in our lives. Some issues have its supernatural side as well as natural side. There needs to be a sense of balance between the supernatural and the natural. Prayer is one of the disciplines of the supernatural but prayer does not rule out or take away our responsibility in the natural. Some results do not come by prayers alone. Man can not do what God alone can do and God in His wisdom will not do what He has empowered man to do on earth. Prayers should not be a cover for work and we should not depend solely on work without prayers.

James 2:26 For as the body without the spirit is dead, so faith without works is dead also.

- **Example 1:** Building the Ark *Genesis 6:14-22.*

  When God instructed Noah to build the ark, He might have shown him where the Gopher wood was and all dimensions needed for the details of the ark. However, God did not get Noah the hammer, saw, nails, and other things needed. Noah had to put these things together.

- **Example 2:** Preparing for Examinations.

  Nehemiah 4:17 Those who built on the wall, and those who carried burdens, loaded themselves so that with one hand they worked at construction, and with the other held a weapon.

Some years ago, a sound Christian lecturer gave us an advice about preparing for examinations, he said: "YOU STUDY FOR EXAMINATIONS AS IF YOU DON'T NEED TO PRAY AND YOU PRAY AS IF YOU DON'T NEED TO STUDY". This approach to examinations ensures success.

- **Example 3:** The Passover in Egypt. *Exodus 11 and 12.*

  God's part: I will pass over the land of Egypt and execute judgement (*Exodus 12:12*)

  Man's Part: The angel of the Lord knows when to pass through the land—it should not be a worry. However, Men would get the lamp (*Exodus 12:3*), do the killing of the lamb (*Exodus 12:6*) and the eating (*Exodus 12:7*). Do not expect the angel of the Lord to kill the lamb, do not expect the angel of the Lord to sprinkle the blood on the door posts. Men had to do these.

- **Example 4:** God's answer to man's heart.

  Proverbs 16:1 The preparations of the heart belong to man, But the answer of the tongue is from the LORD.

  With God things are settled but man needs to prepare and be positioned to receive the answer.

- **Example 5:** Healing of the land.

  2 Chronicles 7:14 If My people who are called by My name will humble themselves, and pray and seek My face, and turn from their wicked ways, then I will hear from heaven, and will forgive their sin and heal their land.

  We can break this verse as follows:

  Man's Part—Decision.

  i.   Humble themselves, pray and seek my face (which man mostly do)

ii. Turn from their wicked ways (God will make grace available but will not force men to turn from their wicked ways)

God's Part—*Result*:

i. God will hear from heaven
ii. Forgive their sins
iii. Heal the land.

Conclusion:

Many people pray and pray (although God applies His mercy and answers), yet we must be ready to play our part—TURN AWAY FROM OUR WICKED WAYS.

It is not surprising that many pray for years and God is yet to heal the land because our part of the equation is incomplete or missing.

- **Example 6:** Finding a life partner.

Proverbs 19:14 Houses and riches are an inheritance from fathers, But a prudent wife is from the LORD.

Proverbs 18:22 He who finds a wife finds a good thing, And obtains favor from the LORD.

There is the story of a young man that prayed for three years because he wanted a good wife! After three years of intense prayers, God instructed the young man to change his ways by learning how to be a good husband and how to be a good father, then He (God) would give him a good wife so he can have a good home.

God does not want to give His 'choice' sons or daughters to rascals. Once you fulfil God's part, be assured that He will keep to His promise too.

- **Example 7:** Securing Strategic Positions.

Nehemiah 4:17 Those who built on the wall, and those who carried burdens, loaded themselves so that with one hand they worked at construction, and with the other held a weapon.

Some people want to be a bank manger, governor, president, judge, minister or aim for other lofty positions. They only pray about it but do not take steps such as hard work, humility, obtain training, networking with relevant people and developing skills in such field of interest.

Several people have lost International job placements and foreign school admissions because they could not produce travelling documents when required. Sadly, I have been one of them.

Others have lost jobs, contracts, properties and other valuables because they do not have the relevant documents to tender at the right time. Learn to put things in place (both natural and supernatural) ahead of time. You might need it sooner than expected. The opportunity once lost may never be regained.

- **Example 8:** Making up the mind.

Romans 12:2 And do not be conformed to this world, <u>but be transformed by the renewing of your mind</u>, that you may prove what is that good and acceptable and perfect will of God.

There are some issues that need to be settled in the mind either before or after prayers so that those issues will not be reoccurring. One could pray about wanting to stop certain bad habits such as immorality, lying or drinking. But there is also the need to make up one's mind about really wanting to stay away from such habits. Several people pray and fast some habits away but they often return to those habits because they have not really made up their minds to quit. The mind needs to be renewed and then a complete transformation can take place.

- **Lots more.**

SIXTEEN

PRAYER AND KNOWLEDGE

After walking with the Lord for awhile, there are some issues you _MAY NO_ longer pray about because of some certain factors such as:

- **Knowledge**

  There are some things that you do not pray for but by virtue of the knowledge you have in God and knowledge in specific areas of life, you get results. Some people just have great knowledge in terms of their finances, some in terms of their health, some in terms of administration and some in terms of relationship. And they apply what they know. Also by virtue of consistent walk with God or other reasons, some areas of our lives can be settled by God's assurance. Unfortunately, there are times when the righteous is not destroyed for lack of prayers but for lack of knowledge. The point being made here is that as soon as we have God's express guidance through His revealed knowledge, we must apply it not asking for what He has already given. The things that are revealed are for us and our children forever.

  Proverbs 11:9b . . . But through knowledge the righteous will be delivered.

  Hosea 4:6 My people are destroyed for lack of knowledge. Because you have rejected knowledge, I also will reject you from being priest for Me; Because you have forgotten the law of your God, I also will forget your children.

Deuteronomy 29:29 The secret things belong to the LORD our God, but those things which are revealed belong to us and to our children forever, that we may do all the words of this law.

John 8:32 And you shall know the truth, and the truth shall make you free

- **Covenant/Principles**

As long as God's covenants or principles are kept, He also keeps His.

Genesis 8:22 While the earth remains, Seedtime and harvest, Cold and heat, Winter and summer And day and night Shall not cease."

Malachi 3:10-11 Bring all the tithes into the storehouse, That there may be food in My house, And try Me now in this Says the LORD of hosts, If I will not open for you the windows of heaven And pour out for you such blessing That there will not be room enough to receive it." And I will rebuke the devourer for your sakes, So that he will not destroy the fruit of your ground, Nor shall the vine fail to bear fruit for you in the field," Says the LORD of hosts;

Example: Hannah honoured her covenant with God by giving Samuel back to the Lord and the Lord opened her womb for other children (*1 Samuel 1-2*)

- **Right Relationship/Friendship**

If you consistently maintain the right relationship with God and people, there are some things you may get even without asking. Sometimes, one may lose material things, but one must ensure valuable relationships are not lost.

A baby does not pray for breast milk from the mother. The mother will give it to the new baby because of the relationship between them and the need of the baby.

Matthew 7:11a If you then, being evil, know how to give good gifts to your children, how much more will your Father who is in heaven give good things to those who ask Him!

Example 1: A paralytic already at the pool of Bethesda *(John 5:1-9)* could not get into the pool because he "had no man" to put him into the water. If he had the right relationships, he would have received assistance into the pool long ago through the help of friends. Jesus would not have met him at the pool if he had friends. However, when we have nobody to support us, Jesus is always there to support us.

Conversely, there was another paralytic who was at home but had friends that ensured he was brought to Jesus through the roof and he got his healing *(Mark 2:1-12)*. God will not come down physically to answer our prayers, He sometimes uses men around us.

Proverbs 18:24 A man who has friends must show himself friendly, But there is a friend who sticks closer than a brother.

Example 2: Mephiboseth, Jonathan's son and Saul's grandson, was a beneficiary of the relationship between David and Jonathan. The relationship enabled him eat at the kings table. He never thought to eat at king David's table. *See 1 Samuel 20:42 and 2 Samuel 9:1, 6-7.*

Example 3: Some people do not pray for jobs or contracts, they only make a phone call to someone in position of control and they swing things in their favour.

For more on friendship get the book HOW TO WIN FRIENDS AND INFLUENCE PEOPLE by Dale Carnegie.

- **Positions, Promotions and Appointments**

There are some benefits that come alongside occupying some positions or being promoted. There are some appointments that are bundled with benefits such as cars, domestic aids, trainings, accommodation and annual vacation. Many people seek the

OTHER THINGS rather than seek the **MAIN THING** that brings **OTHER THINGS**. It happens both in the natural and supernatural.

Matthew 6:33 But seek first the kingdom of God and His righteousness, and all these things shall be added to you.

Example 1: When someone becomes a minister, special adviser, governor, state commissioner, CEO or gets to other lofty positions, all the perquisites of that office will automatically be available and accessible to the individual. They need not be prayed for. The focus of the prayer should be how to attain a desirable position and not the benefits of the position.

• **Maturity and Obedience**

God gives us some things based on our level of maturity with Him and He withholds some things from us when we are not ready for it. He also gives us based on our obedience to Him. He knows we need them and can handle them wisely when given.

John 16:12 "I still have many things to say to you, but you cannot bear them now.

Isaiah 1:19 If you are willing and obedient, you will eat the good of the land;

Job 36: 11-12 If they obey and serve Him, They shall spend their days in prosperity, and their years in pleasures. But if they do not obey, They shall perish by the sword, And they shall die without knowledge.

• **Skills, Gifts and Talents**

Some people have spent time in driving, flying a plane, teaching, repairing cars, cooking or handling specific projects that they have a wealth of experience and have gained mastery in their various fields.

1 Kings 7:13-14 Now king Solomon sent and brought Huram from Tyre. He was the son of a widow from the tribe of Naphtali, and his father was a man of Tyre, a bronze worker; he was filled with wisdom and understanding and skill in working with all kinds of bronze work. So he came to king Solomon and did all his work.

See also 2 Chronicles 2:13-14.

• **Lots more.**

<u>Caution</u>—In as much as we have the above and have developed competence in varying fields, do not depend on it entirely because the arm of flesh can fail. We can not outgrow God's place in our lives. In all circumstances, leave room for the God factor.

Jeremiah 9:23-24 Thus says the Lord "let not the wise man glory in his wisdom, Let not the mighty man glory in his might, Nor let the rich man glory in his riches. But let him who glories glory in this, That he understand and knows Me. That I am the Lord, exercising loving kindness, judgement, and righteousness in the earth. For in this I delight." says the Lord

Proverbs 3:5-6 Trust in the LORD with all your heart, And lean not on your own understanding; In all your ways acknowledge Him, And He shall direct your paths.

SEVENTEEN

PRAYER LEVELS

Just as there are levels in education, finances, relationships, automobile, ministry, evil, faith and many others, there are also levels in prayers.

For the purpose of this book, we will look at five levels of prayer. It can be likened to changing gears in automobiles. However, knowledge is progressive.

- **Level One**: It is like starting up a computer. This is just like making a prayer request. It can also be likened to submitting prayer requests in churches. Some people just wish that they have a request met and it ends there without them pursuing their desire. Sometimes, they don't know how to go about praying.

- **Level Two**: It is like logging into a computer with your login details (username and password). God is checking out if you are serious about the request. You go more than having just a wish to putting action into your desire. God is checking to validate if you are in His records, if you are registered. Are you in the required database?

- **Level Three**: You are fully logged on with little or no rights and privileges. You are praying from the flesh, praying with your body. A level of forgiveness and cleansing for the person praying. A level of gradual separation from the world and its influences. You are praying for the good will of God (*Romans 12:2*)

<u>Example 1</u>: David's prayer as recorded in *Psalm 51* after his wrong dealings

<u>Example 2</u>: Jonah's prayer in the belly of the fish (*Jonah 2*)

- **Level Four**: You are fully logged on with more rights and privileges but you do not have full access yet. You are praying from the mind. There is still some form of distraction. You are praying but your mind is still wandering and bothering with other issues. There is still doubt, there are weights, there is struggle with having the will of God. You are praying for the acceptable will of God (*Romans 12:2*).

<u>Example</u>: Jesus praying in the garden of Gesemene when he was torned between two decisions. *Luke 22:42*.

- **Level Five**: You are fully logged on with all rights and privileges. You are oblivion of your total surrounding. You have full access. You are a super user. You are praying from the spirit. It is a heartfelt prayer. It is deep groaning. Your prayers are fervent or earnest. It may or may not involve speaking in tongues but your spirit, soul and body are aligned with your spirit taking preeminence. Whatever, you ask for at this level is doable. This level also confers an authority on the person praying. He becomes an authority in some areas. There is little or no opposition from the devil. Things happen here. It is a point of encounter. There is a high level of spiritual transaction. This is the realm of the supernatural (where one lives naturally supernatural and supernaturally natural). You are praying the perfect will of God (*Romans 12:2*). This is having God's best in a situation. God is just a thought away. Most people that operate in this level have the baptism of the Holy Spirit in their lives. This is also where the countenance of the person praying may change.

<u>Example 1</u>: When Jesus surrendered His will to God's perfect will, He keyed into the realm of the spirit and was strengthened by angels. *Luke 22: 41-44*

<u>Example 2</u>: Jesus praying on the mount of transfiguration. *Mark 9:2*

<u>Example 3</u>: Elijah's prayer for the release of rain after the heaven was shut for about three years. *1 Kings 18:41-46*

Note: Some details of these levels can not be explained fully as the learning process is continuous. God will move you from one level to another as you allow Him.

EIGHTEEN

PRAYER RESPONSE MEDIA

Here we examine the ways God answers our prayers. When God responds to our prayers, He does so according to our level of walk with Him. He will reach you in a language you can understand as long as your heart is opened to receive His answers.

- **The Bible**

  God answers primarily through His word—the Bible. The Bible remains the best of books. He does nothing that contradicts His word. Do not store the word of God in your head alone but more importantly, store it in your heart by meditation. The more of God's word you store in your spirit, the easier it will be to hear His response to your prayers.

  John 6:63 It is the Spirit who gives life; the flesh profits nothing. The words that I speak to you are spirit, and they are life.

  Psalm 107:20 He sent His word and healed them, And delivered them from their destructions.

  2 Timothy 3:16-17 All Scripture is given by inspiration of God, and is profitable for doctrine, for reproof, for correction, for instruction in righteousness, that the man of God may be complete, thoroughly equipped for every good work.

- **Dreams**

  Don Fleming's Account: *Lets take the account of dreams from the book 'WORLD'S BIBLE DICTIONARY' written by Don Fleming:*[a]

  When God has an important message to pass on, He sometimes spoke to people directly through dreams (*Genesis 20:3, 31:24, 46:2-4, 1 Kings 3:5, Matthew 1:20-24, 2:12*). Among people who do not know God, a dream with meaning usually requires a person who knew God to interpret it (*Genesis 40:9-19, 41:1-32, Daniel 2:1-45, 4:4-27*). Among God's people, a dream with meaning usually had a fairly obvious interpretation (*Genesis 37:5-10, 1 Kings 3:6-9, Acts 16:9-10*).

  Job 33:14-15 For God may speak in one way, or in another, Yet man does not perceive it. In a dream, in a vision of the night, When deep sleep falls upon men, While slumbering on their beds,

  Psalm 16:7 I will bless the Lord who has given me counsel; My heart also instructs me in the night seasons.

  For more on dreams get the book DICTIONARY OF DREAMS by Tella Olayeri.[b]

- **Visions**

  Don Fleming's Account: *Lets take the account of vision from the same book WORLD'S BIBLE DICTIONARY written by Don Fleming*

  Many of the visions mentioned in the Bible seems to be different from dreams (*Genesis 46:2, Job 33:15, Daniel 7:1-2, Acts 16:9*). The main difference seems to be that a dream occurred while a person was asleep, but a vision may have either occurred while a person was either asleep or awake. (*1 Samuel 3:3-15, Psalm 89:19, Daniel 2:19; 8:1-26; 9:20-21, Luke 1:22; Acts 9:10-17; 10:3, 9-17*). Also dream were a common experience among people in general whereas visions are usually given by God to selected people for specific purposes (*Genesis 15:1, 2 Samuel 7:17, Nahum 1:1; Daniel 7:1; 8:1, Acts 11:4-18, 18:9.*)

Daniel 2:19 Then the secret was revealed to Daniel in a night vision. So Daniel blessed the God of heaven

Acts 10:9-16 The next day, as they went on their journey and drew near the city, Peter went up on the housetop to pray, about the sixth hour. Then he became very hungry and wanted to eat; but while they made ready, he fell into a trance[1] and saw heaven opened and an object like a great sheet bound at the four corners, descending to him and let down to the earth. In it were all kinds of four-footed animals of the earth, wild beasts, creeping things, and birds of the air. And a voice came to him, "Rise, Peter; kill and eat." But Peter said, "Not so, Lord! For I have never eaten anything common or unclean." And a voice spoke to him again the second time, "What God has cleansed you must not call common." This was done three times. And the object was taken up into heaven again.

Job 33:14-15 For God may speak in one way, or in another, Yet man does not perceive it. In a dream, in a vision of the night, When deep sleep falls upon men, While slumbering on their beds,

- **God's Still Small Voice**

Isaiah 30:21 Your ears shall hear a word behind you saying, This is the way, walk in it. Whenever you turn to the right hand or whenever you turn to the left

John 10:27 My sheep hear my voice, and I know them, and they follow me:

Elijah got response by a still small voice.

1 Kings 19:11-12 Then He said, "Go out, and stand on the mountain before the LORD." And behold, the LORD passed by, and a great and strong wind tore into the mountains and broke the rocks in pieces before the LORD, but the LORD was not in the wind; and after the wind an earthquake, but the LORD was not in the earthquake; and after the earthquake a fire, but the LORD was not in the fire; and after the fire a still small voice.

John 10:4-5 And when he brings out his own sheep, he goes before them; and the sheep follow him, for they know his voice. Yet they will by no means follow a stranger, but will flee from him, for they do not know the voice of the strangers.

Note: There are some reasons why some Christians do not hear or recognize the 'still small voice'. The reasons include but not limited to the following:

- *One is far from God (God certainly speak)*
- *One is too noisy, busy or the mind is crowded*
- *One needs to grow and mature more in God. Get your spirit man trained and tuned.*
- *One needs to move with people with relatively better experience. An example can be seen between Eli the priest and the little boy Samuel.*
- *Sins and weights*
- *God is still waiting to find you trustworthy in certain areas. You might need to learn how to keep confidences.*
- *Lots more*

- **Brethren or Men of God**

It is very good to be close to people that are spiritual, be close to people that can pick signals from heaven—They can intercede on your behalf and also have answers to some of your prayers. However, as Christians, men of God or brethren should confirm what you already know in your spirit, and this must pass the test of the word of God.

Amos 3:7 Surely the Lord GOD does nothing, Unless He reveals His secret to His servants the prophet

Isaiah 38:1-5 In those days Hezekiah was sick and near death. And Isaiah the prophet, the son of Amoz, went to him and said to him, "Thus says the LORD: 'Set your house in order, for you shall die and not live.' Then Hezekiah turned his face toward the wall, and prayed to the LORD, and said, "Remember now, O LORD, I pray, how I have walked before You in truth and with a loyal heart, and have done what is good in Your sight."

And Hezekiah wept bitterly. And the word of the LORD came to Isaiah, saying, "Go and tell Hezekiah, 'Thus says the LORD, the God of David your father: "I have heard your prayer, I have seen your tears; surely I will add to your days fifteen years.

1 Samuel 1:17 Then Eli answered and said, "Go in peace, and the God of Israel grant your petition which you have asked of Him."

For Christians that are yet to hear directly from God or who want to know the mind of God about a situation, they can confirm from at least two (which agrees with scripture) independent men of God.

Matthew 18:16b . . . 'by the mouth of two or three witnesses every word may be established.

- **Angelic Messages**

  <u>Biblical Examples</u> The visitation and message delivered to *Zacharias in the temple (Luke 1:11-13), Apostle Paul at sea (Acts 27:22-24), Joshua at Canaan (Joshua 5:13-15), John the beloved at Patmos (Revelation 22:16), Balaam on his own way to Balak (Numbers 22:21-35), and many others.*

  Luke 1:11-13 Then the angel of the Lord appeared to him, standing at the right side of the altar of incense. And when Zacharias saw him, he was troubled, and fear fell upon him. But the angel said to him, "Do not be afraid, Zacharias, for your prayer is heard; and your wife Elizabeth will bear you a son, and you shall call his name John.

  <u>Contemporary Example</u> There are people that have angelic visitations and messages from angels even in our days.

  Pastor Roland Buck's Account*: Lets take the account of Pastor Roland Buck from the book ANGELS ON ASSIGNMENT written by Charles and Frances Hunter* [d]

  On the night of June 18, 1978, I went to bed at my usual time with no advance notice that something was about to happen which would change my entire life!

About three o'clock in the morning, I was abruptly awakened when someone grasped my arms and sat me right up in bed! The room was dark because the shades were pulled, but there was just enough light from outside so I could detect the outline of a huge being.

To say the least, I was frightened because he was so strong I couldn't free myself from his grip. My fear didn't last, however, because I quickly became aware of a supernatural presence, and it didn't take me long to realize that this heavenly being was an angel from God. He confirmed this, turned loose of my shoulders, and told me not to be afraid! Then he told me that God had sent him because the prayers of God's people had been heard, and he was to deliver the message that their prayers had not only been heard, but had been answered! Hallelujah! I wasn't dreaming, it wasn't a vision, it was something very, very real!

As we continued talking, he spoke so loudly I was sure he was going to wake up my wife who was asleep next to me. He didn't, but I wish he had!

This unique conversation lasted for two solid hours as the angel shared magnificent truths from the Word of God with me. He discussed the unfolding plan of God for the entire world and brought me warm feelings from God's own heart as to the concern he has for people. His love for people is so great, He is a lot more interested in them than He is in procedure! He LOVES people!

• **Peace of Mind**

It is mostly the case that there will be peace in your inner man when you have answers to some issues. There are exceptions to this rule which is a rare case.

Isaiah 26:3 You will keep him in perfect peace, Whose mind is stayed on You, Because he trusts in You.

- **Revelation Gifts** Word of knowledge, Word of Wisdom and discernment,

  - Word of Knowledge: Spiritual ability to know things in the past and present
  - Word of Wisdom: Spiritual ability to know things in the future
  - Discernment: Knowing the spirit or operation behind a thing. Having good judgement

1 Corinthians 12:8 For to one is given the word of wisdom through the Spirit, to another the word of knowledge through the same Spirit,

- **Prophecy**

  It is one of the gifts of the Holy Spirit. As one progresses in speaking in tongues, one should ask God for the ability to interpret what is being spoken in the spirit. (*1 Corinthians 14:13, 27*). Prophesy is a combination of tongues and interpretation. With prophesy, the church is edified. Prophesies must be backed with scripture. (*1 Corinthians 14:3-5*).

- **Situations Around Us**

  Sometimes happenings around us may or may not be a direct response to prayers, but God just wants to get our attention about some issues. God can speak to you through the trends of things happening around you. Learn to observe the precedents, patterns and trends of things in your family, business, marriage, environment or at specific intervals. He can use nature, animals and many others as deem fit by Him to reach you. He got Balaam's attention through a donkey (Numbers 22:22-34), He snapped Peter back to his senses through a rooster (Matthew 26:74-75), He got Moses attention via the burning bush (Exodus 3:2-4), He got the sailor's attention through storms and they reluctantly flushed Jonah out of the ship after casting lots (Jonah 1) and many others.

- **Lots more.**

NINETEEN

DIFFERENT KINDS OF PRAYER

There are different types of prayers. Knowing how each of them functions enables one to effectively apply them to situation as the need arises.

1 Timothy 2:1 Therefore I exhort first of all that supplications, prayers, intercessions, and giving of thanks be made for all men,

Types of prayers are:

- **Supplication or Prayer of Request**: To ask for help. To bring petition before God. King Hezekiah was being harassed and intimidated by the king of Syria. He just reported the case to God and God handled the case accordingly as recorded in *2 Kings 19:1-37.*

  Matthew 7:7-8 "Ask, and it will be given to you; seek, and you will find; knock, and it will be opened to you. For everyone who asks receives, and he who seeks finds, and to him who knocks it will be opened.

  James 1:5 If any of you lacks wisdom, let him ask of God, who gives to all liberally and without reproach, and it will be given to him.

- **Prayer of Forgiveness, Confession or Repentance**: When you make errors, you had better report to God than allow the devil bring accusations against you. There is no better option with the devil. David is one of the best cases in the Bible. *Psalm 32, 51and 103.*

Proverbs 28:13 He who covers his sins will not prosper, But whoever confesses and forsakes them will have mercy.

James 5:16 Confess your trespasses to one another, and pray for one another, that you may be healed. The effective, fervent prayer of a righteous man avails much.

1 John 1:8-9 If we say that we have no sin we deceive ourselves, and the truth is not in us. If we confess our sins, He is faithful and just to forgive us our sins and to cleanse us from all unrighteousness

Note: If you fall short over a period of time, do not give up on yourself or your struggles, run to His throne of grace and obtain mercy. You can also exchange your weakness for His strength. Also, there is a need to forgive others that have wronged us.

- **Intercession**: To stand in the gap or pray on behalf of others such as family, friends, community, state or country. Being a lawyer or having knowledge of the law can be an added advantage to intercession.

Our greatest intercessor is Jesus

1 Timothy 2:5 For there is one God, and one mediator between God and men, the man Christ Jesus;

Paul interceded for Timothy

2 Timothy 1:3 I thank God, whom I serve with a pure conscience, as my forefathers did, as without ceasing I remember you in my prayers night and day,

Samuel Interceded for Israel

1 Samuel 12:23 Moreover, as for me, far be it from me that I should sin against the LORD in ceasing to pray for you; but I will teach you the good and the right way.

Daniel interceded for Jerusalem *Daniel 9:1-27*

- **Thanksgivings**: Giving thanks for what God has done, giving thanks for what He is currently doing and also giving thanks for what you believe He will yet do.

  Psalm 100:4 Enter into His gates with thanksgiving, and into His courts with praise. be thankful to Him, and bless His name.

  Psalm 95:2 Let us come before his presence with thanksgiving, and shout joyfully to Him with psalms.

  <u>Personal experience:</u> We should also thank God for those things He does on our behalf that we do not have knowledge of. Years ago, I was complaining to God about several things that were lacking in my life. I was very bitter that things were not going as planned. From my point of view, things were going very wrong and God must have had His ears full of my grumbling. However, I gave Him credit for some little things before going to bed. That night God showed me several battles and things He had done on my behalf that I did not have its slightest knowledge. I got out of bed and begged for His forgiveness and mercy. I immediately repented. It is always good to thank God for those things He does on our behalf that we do not even know about.

- **Praise:** Giving honour, respect and adoration to God. When you have a confirmation of an answer from God, just switch into praise even before its manifestation.

  Psalm 150:6 Let everything that has breath praise the LORD. Praise the LORD.

- **Warfare and Deliverance**: To rescue, to redeem, to restore, to buy back. Having a military background or knowing battle strategies can be an added advantage to warfare and deliverance prayers.

1 Timothy 6:12a Fight the good fight of faith,

2 Corinthians 1:10 who delivered us from so great a death, and does deliver us; in whom we trust that He will still deliver us,

Ephesians 6:10-18 Finally, my brethren, be strong in the Lord and in the power of His might. Put on the whole armor of God, that you may be able to stand against the wiles of the devil. For we do not wrestle against flesh and blood, but against principalities, against powers, against the rulers of the darkness of this age, against spiritual hosts of wickedness in the heavenly places. Therefore take up the whole armor of God, that you may be able to withstand in the evil day, and having done all, to stand. Stand therefore, having girded your waist with truth, having put on the breastplate of righteousness, and having shod your feet with the preparation of the gospel of peace; above all, taking the shield of faith with which you will be able to quench all the fiery darts of the wicked one. And take the helmet of salvation, and the sword of the Spirit, which is the word of God; praying always with all prayer and supplication in the Spirit, being watchful to this end with all perseverance and supplication for all the saints—

2 Corinthians 10: 4-5 For the weapons of our warfare are not carnal, but they are mighty in God for pulling down strongholds, casting down arguments and every high thing that exalts itself against the knowledge of God, bringing into captivity to the obedience of Christ

A NOTE ON SPEAKING IN TONGUES

It is praying in an unknown language. It is a spiritual language. It is praying in the spirit. Praying in tongues could either be tongues of men or tongues of angels. (*1 Corinthians 13:1*)

- Tongues of men: Some missionaries often find themselves speaking by supernatural utterance the language of the country where they are carrying out their assignment. The disciples spoke the languages of different nations that were gathered in Jerusalem during Pentecost. *Acts 2:6*

- Tongues of Angels: The host of hell does not understand what the believer is communicating while speaking in tongues. Hence, they can not interrupt the communication because they do not understand it in the first place.

Speaking in tongues comes to the believer mostly during the baptism of the Holy Spirit (*Acts 2:4*). Speaking in tongues is of great value to the believer and should not be taken lightly or abused.

TWENTY

DURATION OF PRAYER

One may ask how long should prayers last? The answer is usually determined by the situations (or issues involved), also the faith or the level of the individual(s) involved amongst other factors.

- Example One—Daniel: *Daniel 10:2-3* The opposition faced by Daniel when he prayed and fasted for 21 days.

- Example Two—Nehemiah: *Nehemiah 2:4* He was before the king and he did not have the luxury of praying long prayers and he also could not afford to make the mistake of making a mistake. The prayers had to be either in seconds or minutes. The king might not even know that Nehemiah had sent a mail (prayer) to the throne of grace and the mail (response) was auto replied with the needed heavenly server (answer).

We must pray until there is a release or confirmation in our hearts. It is strongly recommended that one spends quality time with the LORD in the closet. Spend long hours alone with Him. When this is done, then we can pray short prayers in the open and there will be results. However, spending long hours does not automatically guarantee an answer, but it is certain the spirit man is developed. When faith is in operation, prayer is not long.

If individuals in a group pray consistently, they may not have to spend much time before there is result whenever they come to pray as a group.

Prayer length varies. Some prayers take:

- **<u>Seconds</u>** 'very easy'

Matthew 14:30-31 But when he saw that the wind was boisterous, he was afraid; and beginning to sink he cried out, saying, "Lord, save me!" And immediately Jesus stretched out His hand and caught him, and said to him, "O you of little faith, why did you doubt?"

- **<u>Minutes</u>** 'relatively easy' but sensitivity is sometimes needed.

Nehemiah 2: 4-5 Then the king said to me, "What do you request?" So I prayed to the God of heaven. And I said to the king, "If it pleases the king, and if your servant has found favor in your sight, I ask that you send me to Judah, to the city of my fathers' tombs, that I may rebuild it."

<u>Related experience</u>: One of my mentors told me of a time he was pursuing a big contract with his team, he noticed that everything went wrong during conversation. They were clearly out of favour and all efforts to get approval from the sponsors seemed lost. He was stirred in his spirit to start praying silently and suddenly the tables were turned in their favour during the negotiation.

The import of this testimony is that during some critical moments (such as interviews, interrogations, cross examinations, negotiations, being under attacks or plane going through storms) we must learn to connect to God silently so he can show us where the problem is and the way out.

Luke 12:11-12 "Now when they bring you to the synagogues and magistrates and authorities, do not worry about how or what you should answer, or what you should say. For the Holy Spirit will teach you in that very hour what you ought to say."

Luke 21:15 for I will give you a mouth and wisdom which all your adversaries will not be able to contradict or resist.

- **Hours** 'Getting difficult'

  Matthew 26:39-40 He went a little farther and fell on His face, and prayed, saying, "O My Father, if it is possible, let this cup pass from Me; nevertheless, not as I will, but as You will." Then He came to the disciples and found them sleeping, and said to Peter, "What! Could you not watch with Me one hour?

- **Days** 'Increasingly difficult'

  Daniel 10:2 In those days I, Daniel, was mourning three full weeks.

- **Months** 'For the strong'

  Exodus 24:18 So Moses went into the midst of the cloud and went up into the mountain. And Moses was on the mountain forty days and forty nights.

- **Years** 'Only for people with perseverance'

  Luke 2:37 and this woman was a widow of about eighty-four years, who did not depart from the temple, but served God with fastings and prayers night and day.

TWENTY ONE

NATURAL PRAYER TOOLS

Natural prayer tools are tools viewed from the natural that aid us to pray better or help to jump start praying when we do not feel like praying or too tired to continue praying.

- **Information Technology**: You can send prayer requests and get response from websites or blogs, praying on the phone over a long distance without coming together, praying using chat medium such as yahoo messenger, facebook, yookos, twitter and other social media.

  Daniel 12:4 "But you, Daniel, shut up the words, and seal the book until the time of the end; many shall run to and fro, and knowledge shall increase."

- **Good Administration or Logistics:** Moses would have worn out early if he did not learn to delegate things. *Exodus 18:17-21, Numbers 11:14-17.* Learn to delegate some things so you are free to face more important issues such as praying. Daniel was also able to pray thrice daily because he had friends that could in one way or the other aid his administrative duties (*Daniel 2:48-49*). His prayer life did not make the king's business to suffer.

  Exodus 18:17-21 So Moses' father-in-law said to him, "The thing that you do is not good. Both you and these people who are with you will surely wear yourselves out. For this thing is too much for you; you are not able to perform it by yourself. Listen now to my voice; I will give you counsel, and God will be with you: Stand before God for the people, so that you may bring the difficulties to God. And you shall teach them the statutes and the laws, and show them the way in which they must walk and the work they must do. Moreover you shall select from all the people able men, such as fear God, men of truth, hating covetousness; and place such over them to be rulers of thousands, rulers of hundreds, rulers of fifties, and rulers of tens.

- **Electricity:** In some parts of the world, electricity supply is not constant. Where it is available, it becomes a veritable tool as it enables the praying person to read the Bible and pray effectively.

- **Right Feeding**: Knowing when to eat, what to eat, quality of food and the quantity of food makes you healthy and light to be able to pray especially at night or to get up very early to pray. Some persons feel very heavy at night if they either eat late or eat heavily. Some people have nightmares when they eat late or heavily. Know your body system and stick to what works best for you.

Ecclesiastes 10:16-17 Woe to you, O land, when your king is a child, And your princes feast in the morning! Blessed are you, O land, when your king is the son of nobles, And your princes feast at the <u>proper time</u>—

- **A little Coffee**: When you are very tired, (may be after a hard day work or schedule), you can kick up with a little coffee. But seek medical clearance before taking coffee as it does have its aftermath effect on some individuals.

- **Good Rest**: When the body is well rested and the mind is cleared, one can key into prayer with a disciplined mind or spirit.

- **Bath**: It is good to pray when you are fresh, maybe in the morning. Some people can have a bath at night or midnight and hence they become fresh. Taking bath is a therapy on its own as it gives one strength to pray. I have experienced this several times.

- **Good Accommodation**: A good environment allows praying consistently with the least amount of distraction. It limits troubles. A room was made available for Elisha by the shunammite woman

2 kings 4:10 Please, let us make a small upper room on the wall; and let us put a bed for him there, and a table and a chair and a lampstand; so it will be, whenever he comes to us, he can turn in there."

- **Mobile Accommodation**: You can invite God into your vehicle by playing spiritual music when in transit or when the traffic is heavy. Once you alight, you are already tuned and will not feel too tired to pray.

- **Education, Exposure, Experience**: Experience does not come with age alone but more with frequency or intensity of usage. You can leverage on your past experiences but do not depend too much on it as changes do occur.

- **Natural knowledge in Various Areas**: You pray for your health but also have a doctor for medical care. You pray for your car but have a mechanic to fix things. You pray for your academics but also have knowledge about the area to study for examinations.

Proverbs 11:9b But through knowledge the righteous will be delivered.

John 8:32 And you shall know the truth, and the truth shall make you free.

- **Mentors and Coaches**: You can not take lightly the counsel of people that have been where you are going. Someone sees what you do not see. Someone knows what you need to know. Someone has what will benefit you. They help you soften the soil. You may gain in a year from such association what you may not get after spending ten years of self effort. Develop such association and do not take their counsel for granted. It helps to have spiritual mentors.

2 Kings 3:11But Jehoshaphat said, "Is there no prophet of the LORD here, that we may inquire of the LORD by him?" So one of the servants of the king of Israel answered and said, "Elisha the son of Shaphat is here, who poured water on the hands of Elijah.

- **Living on schedule or Use of Daytime Reminders**: Setting an alarm (clocks, watches or phones) for specific times can help to put one in schedule for a while and serve as reminders. After awhile of being consistent with the schedule, the body adapts to praying without any alarm.

- **Morning Cry**: Some environments have men and women that constantly ring bells, sing choruses, and announce to everyone to rise from bed to pray. They are referred to as morning criers in my part of the world. They can serve as positive tools for prayers.

- **Lots more.**

TWENTY TWO

SPIRITUAL PRAYER TOOLS

Spiritual tools are tools that enable us to pray better from a spiritual point of view. Some of the tools include:

- **Relationship with God:** God created every man. Everyman has a relationship with God on the basis of CREATOR to CREATURE. However, as we develop deeper relationship, it becomes much easier to commune with God in prayer. The closer we are to God, the better He responds to our prayers.

  John 15:4-5 Abide in Me, and I in you. As the branch cannot bear fruit of itself, unless it abides in the vine, neither can you, unless you abide in Me. "I am the vine, you are the branches. He who abides in Me, and I in him, bears much fruit; for without Me you can do nothing.

  James 4:8a Draw near to God and He will draw near to you.

- **Praying According to God's Will:** Praying in the wrong direction makes prayer ineffective but when we pray aright like Solomon did in Gibeon, God answers speedily.

  James 4:3 You ask and do not receive, because you ask amiss, that you may spend it on your pleasures.

  See also 1 kings 3:10-14

- **Praying in the Spirit:** Helps us pray aright in a given situation.

  Romans 8:26, Likewise the Spirit also helps in our weaknesses. For we do not know what we should pray for as we ought, but the Spirit Himself makes intercession for us with groanings which cannot be uttered.

  Jude 1:20 But you, beloved, building yourselves up on your most holy faith, praying in the Holy Spirit,

- **God's Word/Reading, Studying, and Meditation:** Pray inline with the word of God and personalize it. When one spends quality time reading, afterwards studying and finally in meditation, praying becomes effortless.

  Colossians 3:16 Let the word of Christ dwell in you richly in all wisdom, teaching and admonishing one another in psalms and hymns and spiritual songs, singing with grace in your hearts to the Lord.

- **Faith:** When faith is in operation, prayer is not usually long.

  Mark 11:23-24 For assuredly, I say to you, whoever says to this mountain, 'Be removed and be cast into the sea, and does not doubt in his heart, but believes that those things he says will be done, he will have whatever he says Therefore I say to you, whatever things you ask when you pray, believe that you receive them, and you will have them.

- **Righteousness:** The Lord loves the righteous and hears their cry, however, our righteousness is not the main reason why God answers our prayers but according to his grace and sovereignty.

  Psalm 34:17 The righteous cry out, and the LORD hears, And delivers them out of all their troubles.

- **Fasting:** Fasting gives wings to prayers.

  Mark 9:29 So He said to them, "This kind can come out by nothing but prayer and fasting."

- **Humility:** He gives grace to the humble and resists the proud. The humble in heart will gain access into His presence.

  Psalm 51:17: the sacrifices of the God are a broken spirit, a broken and contrite heart These, God, You will not despite

  1 Peter 5:6 Therefore humble yourselves under the mighty hand of God, that He may exalt you in due time,

- **Godly music:** Music is a prayerful tool when used godly.

  Colossians 3:16 Let the word of Christ dwell in you richly in all wisdom, teaching and admonishing one another in psalms and hymns and spiritual songs, singing with grace in your hearts to the Lord.

- **Lots more.**

TWENTY THREE

PRAYER AND FASTING

Isaiah 58:1-14 "Cry aloud, spare not; Lift up your voice like a trumpet; Tell My people their transgression, And the house of Jacob their sins. Yet they seek Me daily, And delight to know My ways, As a nation that did righteousness, And did not forsake the ordinance of their God. They ask of Me the ordinances of justice; They take delight in approaching God.' Why have we fasted,' they say, 'and You have not seen? Why have we afflicted our souls, and You take no notice?' "In fact, in the day of your fast you find pleasure, And exploit all your laborers. Indeed you fast for strife and debate, And to strike with the fist of wickedness. You will not fast as you do this day, To make your voice heard on high. Is it a fast that I have chosen, A day for a man to afflict his soul? Is it to bow down his head like a bulrush, And to spread out sackcloth and ashes? Would you call this a fast, And an acceptable day to the LORD?" Is this not the fast that I have chosen: To loose the bonds of wickedness, To undo the heavy burdens, To let the oppressed go free, And that you break every yoke? Is it not to share your bread with the hungry, And that you bring to your house the poor who are cast out; When you see the naked, that you cover him, And not hide yourself from your own flesh? Then your light shall break forth like the morning, Your healing shall spring forth speedily, And your righteousness shall go before you; The glory of the LORD shall be your rear guard. Then you shall call, and the LORD will answer; You shall cry, and He will say, 'Here I am.' "If you take away the yoke from your midst, The pointing of the finger, and speaking wickedness, If you extend your soul to the hungry And satisfy the afflicted soul, Then your light shall dawn in the darkness, And your darkness shall be as the noonday. The LORD will guide you continually, And satisfy your soul in drought, And strengthen your bones; You shall be like a watered garden, And like a spring of water, whose waters do not fail. Those from among you Shall build the old waste places; You shall raise up the foundations of many generations; And you shall be called the Repairer of the Breach, The Restorer of Streets to Dwell In. "If you turn away your foot from the Sabbath, From doing your pleasure on My holy day, And call the Sabbath a delight, The holy day of the LORD honorable, And shall honor Him, not doing your own ways, Nor finding your own pleasure, Nor speaking your own words, Then you shall delight yourself in the LORD; And I will cause you to ride on the high hills of the earth, And feed you with the heritage of Jacob your father. The mouth of the LORD has spoken."

<u>Prayer and Fasting</u>: fasting is the abstinence from food and pleasures so as to be tuned into the realm of the spirit. Fasting can also be defined as the act of crucifying or subduing the flesh so that our spirit man is tuned to link up with God. Some situations are very stubborn and must be supported with fasting for solutions. Fasting can be said to be a catalyst to prayer.

Mark 9:29 So He said to them, "This kind can come out by nothing but prayer and fasting."

The duration of fasting can be eight hours, one day, two days, three days, five days, seven days, ten days, fourteen days, twenty one days, forty days, hundred days, one hundred and twenty days and so on.

Fasting is not doing God any favour, but a spiritual exercise, pummelling the flesh and elevating the spirit to be more focused.

There are different **types of fasting** such as

- <u>Daily fasting</u>: From evening to evening. You break every day

- <u>Partial fasting</u>: Fruits and water only, or abstinence from some kinds of food.

- <u>Dry fasting</u>: No food or water. Some refer to it as marathon fasting.

A long fast is a fast that spans for three days without food or water. It can also span more than three days with or without water.

<u>Points to note before embarking on long fasts</u>: It should be well planned and adequate preparation made. The different areas of preparation include:

- <u>Spiritual Preparation</u>: Before embarking on a long fast, make sure you are spirit led.

- <u>Mental Preparation</u>: It is good one has the end in mind before any venture. Fasting is not an exception. Have a determined mind. Know the reason why you are fasting and not just for 'show'. Count the cost.

- <u>Medical or Physical Preparation</u>: Before the start of the fast, you may begin to regulate the quantity of food. In other words, you begin to 'SLOW DOWN' before commencing a fast. Eat fresh vegetables, fruits or take fish pepper soup. It is also a good idea to seek medical clearance if your body system can withstand the fasting period (exercise). A Christian medical doctor once said most people with ulcers are Christians that do not know how to handle fasting properly. Please, seek medical clearance.

- <u>Environments:</u> You may require a very quiet place devoid of noise and distractions and also having good ventilation.

- <u>Notification:</u> In as much as it is strongly advisable that you keep it to yourself, there are some exceptions such as for married couples—it is advisable you keep your partner in the know of your fast for understandable reasons. Also, if you have some secular duties, you may proceed on leave or inform someone that will stand in for you. You may also relate with someone who has better experience so as to receive invaluable information.

- <u>Draw up a schedule or Plan:</u> An example of a schedule could be

    o   Hours of prayers,
    o   Hours of meditation,
    o   Christian books to read,
    o   Time to be still or silent

o Audio books to listen to

o Specific area of focus which is determined by the reason for fasting.

o Lots more

- Lots more.

POINTS TO NOTE DURING LONG FASTS:

- The body might be weak but give time to great meditation (The word of God).
- The body might be weak but give quality time to prayers
- Follow your schedule but allow for flexibility without loosing focus.
- Have a pen and writing material handy to take notes of instructions
- Temptation should be expected but you can overcome. Jesus overcame and if you believe the things He did you also will overcome *John 14:12*
- Whenever the body becomes very weak, it is a transition stage, you will resume with inner strength sooner or later.
- Your urine will change, your saliva will become thick or your mouth may smell.
- Look cheerful and radiant. Apply oil on your face or use mouth spray if you are involved in meetings with people.
- Don't be distracted by the time being 'SLOW'. It will apparently appear slow.
- You may have people that you pray together.
- Accountability to someone of better experience (godly and wise counsel)
- Lots more.

POINTS TO NOTE ABOUT BREAKING LONG FASTS:

Long fasts are not as tough as breaking the fasts. You must break with caution:

- If you have been fasting for a long time, the same discipline should make you 'SLOW DOWN' when breaking so as not to complicate your systems. Many of us learnt it the very hard way. Learn to break very slowly

- Break with light foods such as fruits, vegetables and pepper soup or Holy Communion. DO NOT EAT HEAVILY—you may be inviting trouble for your systems.

- As you break slowly, it takes about half of the duration of your fast to return to your normal feeding routine.

  Examples: A fast of seven days, takes breaking gradually for about three and half days to return to normal. Likewise, fasting for twenty-one days, takes about ten days to get back to your normal eating routine.

- If your system is troubled, resume fasting or start the process again. Your system will correct itself, afterwards break properly.

- If you develop complication, which is rare, seek competent medical help.

NOTABLE FASTS IN THE BIBLE INCLUDE:

- **Moses:** *Exodus 24:15-18; 34:28*
- **David:** *2 Samuel 12:16-18*
- **Jonah:** *Jonah 1:17, Jonah 3:5-10*
- **Daniel:** *Daniel 10:2-3*
- **Nehemiah:** *Nehemiah 1:4*
- **Ezra:** *Ezra 8:21-23*
- **Esther:** *Esther 4:15-16*
- **Jesus:** *Matthew 4:2*
- **Elijah:** *2 kings 19:7-8*
- **Paul:** *Acts 9:9*
- **Lots more.**

THE REWARDS OF FASTING INCLUDE:

- Boost to prayers.

- Self Control/Discipline: It may help you stop some bad habits especially after three days dry fast.

- Spiritual growth.

- Biological effects such as healing of the body through cleansing.

- Manifestation of Spiritual gifts such as discernment of spirit, power gifts and more.

- Ministering and deliverance becomes easier.

- Lots more.

Note: Start small with half a day fast and develop over time.

TWENTY FOUR

WHEN TO START AND STOP PRAYING

A. WHEN TO START PRAYING

Generally, we are never to stop praying as the word of God admonishes us to pray without ceasing (*1 Thessalonians 5:17*). However we should start praying or re-enforce our prayers when:

1. **Our Spirit Man is Troubled or Burdened**: We need to pull aside and pray, it could just be an invitation to prayer

    Example: Jesus before facing the cross

    Matthew 26:38-39 Then He said to them, My soul is exceedingly sorrowful, even to death. Stay here and watch with Me. He went a little further and fell on His face, and prayed, saying, O My Father, if it is possible, let his cup pass over Me; nevertheless not my will, but as You will.

2. **Faced with Dangerous Situations**

    Example: Peter called Jesus to save him from drowning.

    Matthew 14:30-31 But when he saw that the wind was boisterous, he was afraid; and beginning to sink he cried out, saying, "Lord, save me!" And immediately Jesus stretched out His hand and caught him, and said to him, "O you of little faith, why did you doubt?"

3. **Before Taking Life's Major Decisions:** There are some things our physical eyes cannot see nor do our human minds comprehend. You must pray and ensure that you are in the center of His will by keying into the spirit. Many destinies would not have been aborted if much prayers and preparation have been embarked upon before taking on some major life's decisions. Some of the major decisions include but not limited to:

- *Choosing a life partner:* It is strongly recommended to start praying before you meet the person you intend to marry. You can love everyone but you cannot marry just anyone. There are several factors that interplay to determine who you marry. Marriage can make or mar your productivity in life. There are several people that want a divorce but they are afraid of what the church and people around them would say, which implies that they are not enjoying what they entered into. There is an increase in divorce cases annually. The best thing is to get it right from the drawing board. May you not make a mistake of marrying a mistake in Jesus name. Amen.

   Proverbs 18:22 He who finds a wife finds a good thing, And obtains favor from the LORD.

- *Close Associates:* Jesus prayed a lot before choosing His disciples; Likewise, much prayer is needed before choosing business partners, visions carriers and other aides around you. You need heaven's clearance before getting close to some people. Not everyone can have an active part in your future. Take time to trust people and verify their trust periodically. May you not be close to people that you have no business with. May you not be close to vision killers and dream stealers and people that do not have your interest at heart. May God reveal your false friends and true enemies to you. Amen
   Mark 3:13-14 And He went up on the mountain and called to Him those He Himself wanted. And they came to Him. Then He appointed twelve, that they might be with Him and that He might send them out to preach,

- *Relocating:* God told Abraham to move out of the land where he was. On the contrary, God told his son, Isaac, not to move but stay in the land where he was. Abraham that moved out got blessed, likewise Isaac that stayed also got blessed. With much praying and an open mind, you will have God's specific direction for you—whether you travel abroad or stay where you are. You do not have to join the band wagon. God knows where you can flourish best. God's direction will always be for your profit and progress.

  Psalm 32:8 I will instruct and teach you in the way you should go; I will guide you with My eye.

- *Career, Jobs, Purpose or Callings:* Many people are doing jobs and are involved in careers that they are not crafted for. Getting in touch with God makes you know His purpose and His calling for your life. May you not be busy in the wrong direction in Jesus name. Amen

  Proverbs 3:5-6 Trust in the LORD with all your heart, And lean not on your own understanding; In all your ways acknowledge Him, And He shall direct your paths.

  Psalm 37:4-6 Delight yourself also in the LORD, And He shall give you the desires of your heart. Commit your way to the LORD, Trust also in Him, And He shall bring it to pass. He shall bring forth your righteousness as the light, And your justice as the noonday.

- *Inestimable Projects or Large Business Ventures:* Projects such as building the walls of Jerusalem under the supervision of Nehemiah should not be taken lightly. When the risk involved in an enterprise is large and you do not even know all the oppositions you will face, much prayer is needed before starting and tact is needed during execution. There are some appointments that require getting clearance from above before acceptance.

  Psalm 61:2 From the end of the earth I will cry to You, When my heart is overwhelmed; Lead me to the rock that is higher than I.

- *Other Life's major decisions.*

4. **When we do not Understand Some Issues** There are some issues such as having a bad dream that you do not understand its meaning or a dream that you can not even recollect clearly, it could be an invitation to prayer and God will reach you at your level because He speaks to His loved ones in a language they will understand despite their level of walk with Him.

   Matthew 11:28 Come to Me, all you who labor and are heavy laden, and I will give you rest.

5. **When You Have Just Won a Battle or After a Victory:** When battles are won, it is normal to relax. Victory often invites and stirs up unknown opposition. However, this is not the best of time to relax, its a time to pull aside and pray.

Example: Jesus would always pull aside to pray after a major victory.

   Matthew 14:19-23 Then He commanded the multitudes to sit down on the grass. And He took the five loaves and the two fish, and looking up to heaven, He blessed and broke and gave the loaves to the disciples; and the disciples gave to the multitudes. So they all ate and were filled, and they took up twelve baskets full of the fragments that remained. Now those who had eaten were about five thousand men, besides women and children. Immediately Jesus made His disciples get into the boat and go before Him to the other side, while He sent the multitudes away. And when He had sent the multitudes away, He went up on the mountain by Himself to pray. Now when evening came, He was alone there.

6. **Lots more.**

B. WHEN TO STOP PRAYING

Generally, we are never to stop praying as the word of God admonishes us to pray without ceasing. However, there are some exceptions when we might need to stop praying over a particular issue.

1. **When God Answers** Sometimes God has answered but we do not see the manifestation immediately.

   Example *Acts 12:5, 7, 13-16.* Peter was imprisoned by Herod, prayers were offered by the disciples on his behalf. The prayer was answered and he was released by an angel, He went to where the disciples where gathered and funny enough they were still praying (making a request) for what God had already answered. Perhaps, they should have changed their prayer from request to thanksgiving. So we may not stop praying on other issues but there is no point requesting what has already been supplied.

2. **When There is Peace** *Mark 4:39* Peace brings about a confirmation in our inner man. If we are sure that God has given us peace over an issue, we can only go ahead to thank Him.

   Isaiah 26:3 You will keep him in perfect peace, whose mind is stayed on You, because he trusts in You.

3. **When There is Instruction From the Lord**

   Example 1: Joshua

   Once there is an instruction from the Lord, following the instruction guarantees solution.

   Joshua 7:10-12 So the LORD said to Joshua: "Get up! Why do you lie thus on your face? Israel has sinned, and they have also transgressed My covenant which I commanded them. For they have even taken some of the accursed things, and have both stolen and deceived; and they have also put it among their own stuff. Therefore the children of Israel could not stand before their enemies, but turned their backs before their enemies, because they have become doomed to destruction. Neither will I be with you anymore, unless you destroy the accursed from among you.

   Example 2: Moses

   There is a time to pray and there is a time to act.

Exodus 14:15 And the LORD said to Moses, "Why do you cry to Me? Tell the children of Israel to go forward.

4. Continual disobedience to God's Instructions: *See Jeremiah 7:1-16*

Jeremiah 7:16 Therefore do not pray for this people, nor lift up a cry or prayer for them, nor make intercession to Me; for I will not hear you.

At our initial walk with God, He begins to give us instructions to obey from His word (Bible). For a while, He would overlook our wrong doings. After a while, when we continually and deliberately disobey God's instructions, He would not take it lightly again because He expects us to obey. It will be a waste of time and energy praying. At such time, we had rather get back on track or risk His judgement.

However, when we do not deliberately disobey God's instructions and are very sincere about amending our ways, we should run to Him for grace and we would receive His mercy and strength.

5. Lots more.

Pastor Sunday Adelaja's Account*: Below is an account of when to stop praying from Pastor Sunday Adelaja's book, CHURCH SHIFT* [a]

Sometimes people pray without ever taking action. There is a time to leave the prayer room and carry out the plans God has revealed to you. For too many years some Christians have concentrated on prayer only. They believe that God will supernaturally accomplish what they are asking for. But the word of God says faith without works is useless and dead, according to James 2:17. The kingdom does not advance on prayers alone, but on prayer-inspired actions.

You will recall that when our church was needing a permanent place to meet, we prayed for a year and God was silent. That silence bothered me terribly. I couldn't understand why we had prayed and God hadn't done anything. I was still expecting God to do everything for us. I wasn't putting my faith into action. Finally, God had mercy on me and told me that prayer doesn't do anything by itself. "No matter how you pray, it is not in My hands," God spoke to my heart. "The solution is in your hands. I have given you the opportunity. The people of the world don't understand prayer. They understand the language of force. Prayer is for me and this is not My situation. It is within your scope of influence to change it. You are on the earth; you have the people and you have the power. Use your power."

It was time for us to quit praying, and we did. Our actions led to favorable resolution to our problem and eventually led to a change in the entire nation. But many people still cling to old ways. They are almost idolatrous in prayer.

TWENTY FIVE

BIBLICAL PRAYER LEGENDS

There are several Biblical prayer legends which include: Moses, Elijah, Jesus, Nehemiah, Esther, David, Paul, Daniel and many more.

We would examine the prayer life of three people in the Bible. The three to be examined are: Moses, Daniel and Jesus Christ.

A.   PRAYER LIFE OF MOSES

If there was ever a man that had a close relationship with God in the Old Testament, then that man was Moses. He is referred to as the deliverer of Israel from the bondage in Egypt. He devoted himself to prayer so much that God spoke to him face to face. God's response to Moses' prayers were not in dark sayings but in plain language (*Numbers 12:6-8*).

He earlier thought he could use his natural strength and military experience to deliver the children of Israel from Egypt but God had to 'DE-PROGRAME' and afterwards 'RE-PROGRAMME' his spirit and his mind in the wilderness. He had to drop many things he learned in the palace and learnt new things in the wilderness. The unlearning and learning process took him about forty years. The wilderness experience developed the prayer life of Moses. He had been in the palace for forty years so God had to re-orientate him for another forty years.

His prayer life was more of solitude in the wilderness and mountain tops. He constantly enjoyed God's presence and he could listen attentively and see issues clearly during his separation for prayers. His spending quality time alone with God affected the continuance of his face. One can note that climbing the mountains every morning to pray is also a form of physical exercise for his body. The prayer life of Moses made him enjoy God's presence. No wonder he was still strong in old age.(*Deuteronomy 34:7*).

B. PRAYER LIFE OF DANIEL

One of the spiritual disciplines in the life of Daniel is prayer. Other disciplines include fasting, worship, scripture meditation, service and spiritual association.

Daniel was away from his place of birth and there was no church (temple) in Babylon-a good excuse to abandon prayer and other spiritual disciplines.

Although, he was taken away with others at an early age, He knew that he was in Babylon but not of Babylon. He separated himself from the influence in Babylon but did not isolate himself from events in Babylon. He alongside, Shadrach, Meshach, and Abed-Nego, participated in happenings in Babylon and secured positions in public administration.

Through prayer, dreams and visions were revealed to him at night. Prayer became a way of life to Daniel and he prayed thrice daily despite being the vice-president of the world's super power of his time. He prayed despite targeted laws against prayer and the God whom he served continually delivered him from the lion's den. He also interceded for the restoration of Jerusalem. The prayer life of Daniel points to the fact that a consistent prayer life will result in an overall disciplined life.

C. PRAYER LIFE OF JESUS CHRIST

Prayer is part of the make up of our Lord Jesus Christ. Jesus observed times of prayer (*Mark 1:35. Luke 6:12*). He would get up early before dawn to pray or He would be praying through out the night. He would not take a major decision without quality time in prayers. For instance, He prayed before appointing the twelve apostles and before His trial and crucifixion.

Nothing happened to Jesus unawares because he was in constant touch with the father. What He sees the Father do, that is what He does. After feeding the multitudes, He separated Himself into a solitary place to pray. He will not neglect prayers even after a major victory.

Jesus knelt to pray and also paced when praying. Sometimes the intensity of the prayer could make His sweat become blood. He was soaked in prayers.

One of the several benefits of prayer in the life of Jesus was that He could accomplish His purpose on earth within the time frame. Jesus did in thirty three years what no one else has been able to do in a lifetime.

TWENTY SIX

CONTEMPORARY PRAYER LEGENDS

There are several contemporary prayer legends which include but not limited to Maria Woodworth Etter, Smith Wigglesworth, Joseph Babalola, Dr. Daniel Olukoya, Sunday Adelaja, Pastor E.A. Adeboye, Martin Luther, Henry F. Lyte, Archbishop Benson Idahosa, Praying Hyde, Susana Wesley to mention a few. You can be one of these if only you can pay the price.

We will take three contemporary legends to be a source of challenge and encouragement, the others can be searched out and there are several others that are better known to God. The three to be mentioned are: Smith Wigglesworth, Joseph Babalola and Sunday Adelaja.

A. SMITH WIGGLESWORTH (1859-1947)

I don't often spend more than half an hour in prayer at one time, but I never go more than half an hour without praying—*Smith Wigglesworth*

1. **_Roberts Liardon's Account_**: *Lets take the account of Smith Wigglesworth by Roberts Liardon from the book GOD'S GENERALS* [a]

   Smith Wigglesworth was born in 1859 to a very poor family. His father did manual labour, for very little pay. Smith himself went to work at the age of six to help with the family income. At six he was pulling turnips and at seven he was working in a woolen mill twelve hours a day. His parents did not know God, but Smith hungered in his heart to know Him. Even as a youngster he would pray in the fields. His grandmother was the critical Christian in his life. She was a Weslyan Methodist and would take Smith to meetings with her. At one of these meetings there was a song being sung about Jesus as the lamb and Smith came into the realization of God's love for him and his decision to believe Christ for his salvation was decided that day. He was immediately filled with the desire to evangelize and led his own mother to Christ.

Smith had various church experiences as he was growing up. He first went to an Episcopal church and then at thirteen a Weslyan Methodist church. When he was sixteen he became involved in the Salvation Army. He felt deeply called to fast and pray for lost souls. He saw many people come to Christ. At seventeen a mentor shared with him about water baptism and he decided to be baptized. The Salvation Army was experiencing a tremendous level of the power of God in those days. He describes meetings where "many would be prostrated under the power of the Spirit, sometimes for as long as twenty-four hours at a time." They would pray and fast and cry out for the salvation of fifty or a hundred people for the week and they would see what they had prayed for.

At eighteen Smith left the factory and became a plumber. He moved to Liverpool when he was twenty and continued to work during the day and minister during his free time. He felt called to minister to young people and brought them to meetings. These were destitute and ragged children, whom he would often feed and care for. Hundreds were saved. Smith was often asked to speak in Salvation meetings and he would break down and weep under the power of God. Many would come to repentance in those meetings through this untrained man. At twenty-three he returned back Bradford and continued his work with the Salvation Army.

In Bradford Smith met Mary Jane Featherstone, known as Polly, which later culminated into marriage

The couple worked together to evangelize the lost. They opened a small church in a poor part of town. Polly would preach and Smith would make the altar calls. For a season, however, Smith became so busy with his plumbing work that his evangelistic fervor began to wane. Polly continued on, bringing Smith to conviction. One day while Smith was working in the town of Leeds he heard of a divine healing meeting. He shared with Polly about it. She needed healing and so they went to a meeting, and Polly was healed.

Smith struggled with the reality of healing, while being ill himself. He decided to give up the medicine that he was taking and trust God. He was healed. They had five children, a girl and four boys. One morning two of the boys were sick. The power of God came and they prayed for the boys and they were instantly healed. Smith struggled with the idea that God would use him to heal the sick in general. He would gather up a group of people and drive them to get prayer in Leeds. The leaders of the meeting were going to a convention and left Smith in charge. He was horrified. How could he lead a meeting about divine healing? He tried to pass it off to someone else but could not. Finally he led the meeting and several people were healed. That was it. From then on Smith began to pray for people for healing.

Smith had another leap to make. He had heard about the Pentecostals who were being baptized in the Holy Spirit. He went to meetings and was so hungry for God he created a disturbance and church members asked him to stop. He went to prayer and prayed for four days. Finally he was getting ready to head home and the vicar's wife prayed for him and he fell under the power of God and spoke in tongues. Everything changed after that. He would walk by people and they would come under the conviction of the Holy Spirit and be saved. He began to see miracles and healings and the glory of God would fall when he prayed and preached.

Smith had to respond to the many calls that came in and gave up his business for the ministry. Polly unexpectedly died in 1913, and this was a real blow to Smith. He prayed for her and commanded that death release her. She did arise but said "Smith—the Lord wants me." His heartbroken response was "If the Lord wants you, I will not hold you". She had been his light and joy for all the years of their marriage, and he grieved deeply over the loss. After his wife was buried he went to her grave, feeling like he wanted to die. When God told him to get up and go Smith told him only if you "give to me a double portion of the Spirit—my wife's and my own—I would go and preach the Gospel. God was gracious to me and answered my request." His daughter Alice and son-in-law James Salter began to travel with him to handle his affairs.

Smith would pray and the blind would see, and the deaf were healed, people came out of wheelchairs, and cancers were destroyed. One remarkable story is when He prayed for a woman in a hospital. While he and a friend were praying she died. He took her out of the bed stood her against the wall and said "in the name of Jesus I rebuke this death". Her whole body began to tremble. The he said "in the name of Jesus walk", and she walked. Everywhere he would go he would teach and then show the power of God. He began to receive requests from all over the world. He taught in Europe, Asia, New Zealand and many other areas. When the crowds became very large he began a "wholesale healing". He would have everyone who needed healing lay hands on themselves and then he would pray. Hundreds would be healed at one time.

Throughout Smith's ministry it was confirmed that 14 people were raised from the dead. Thousands were saved and healed and he impacted whole continents for Christ. Smith died on March 12, 1947 at the funeral of his dear friend Wilf Richardson. His ministry was based on four principles:" First, read the Word of God. Second, consume the Word of God until it consumes you. Third believe the Word of God. Fourth, act on the Word."

2. **_Dr. Lester Sumrall's Account:_** *Let take the account of Smith Wigglesworth by Dr. Lester Sumrall (who knew Wigglesworth personally) in his book called "PIONEERS OF FAITH.*[b]

Someone once asked Smith Wigglesworth how he gets up in the morning. This is what he said:

'I jump out of bed! I dance before the Lord for at least ten to twelve minutes—high-speed dancing. I jump up and down and run around my room telling God how great He is, how wonderful He is, how glad I am to be associated with Him and to be His child.'

After this, he would take a cold shower, read the Bible for an hour, pray for an hour, then open his mail to see what God would have him do that day. He was an extremely remarkable man, totally sold out to God.

3. **Another account of his praying** *in a restaurant by Dr. Lester Sumrall (who knew Wigglesworth personally) from the same book called* "PIONEERS OF FAITH." '

"The pastor told me, 'Smith Wigglesworth was here in my city recently, and I took him to one of the fanciest restaurants to have lunch on Sunday. When we came into the restaurant, someone took his coat and hung it up for him. He looked around like an eagle. Only wealthy people ate in this restaurant. Instead of sitting down, he took a fork and began to hit the side of his glass with it. BING! BING! BING! BING! Everybody stopped eating.

When he had everybody's attention, he raised his hand and said, 'Ladies and gentlemen, I have noticed since arriving here that none of you prayed over your food. You resemble a bunch of hogs to me. You just jump in and eat without giving thanks to the One Who provided it for you. Bow your heads and I'll pray for you.'

'Wigglesworth raised his hands and prayed for those people. Before we left the restaurant, two families came over and got saved.

4. **Another account of his praying** *started by Jeff in his blog,* [d]

"Wigglesworth, A Man Who Walked with God." It was written by a man who knew Smith well. In this book, he tells how that Wigglesworth used to have prayer sessions where the power of God was so strong, that Wigglesworth was sometimes the only . . . person left in the room. One minister said that, if he ever had the chance to be in one of those meetings, he was not going to leave. He was going to stay there after everybody else was gone, because he wanted to see what Wigglesworth was experiencing. He was invited to one of these sessions, and he described the presence of God that came into the room. He said that it was so powerful, that one by one the ministers began to leave. He was determined to remain. He said that finally he found himself on the floor, weeping uncontrollably. Wigglesworth, on the other hand, was still standing with his hands raised, praying and praising God. This man said that he finally had to leave. He said, "I knew that if I stayed in that room any longer, I would die."

B. JOSEPH AYO BABALOLA (1904-1959)

1. **_Rev S.A Sadela's Account:_** *Lets take the account of the prayer life of Joseph Ayo Babalola as attested by Rev S.A Sadela, President/Founder, Gospel Apostolic Church* [e]

His Prayer and Fasting

Right from the beginning of his ministry Apostle Babalola lived a life given to much prayer and fasting. He would go on without food or water for 3 days, 7 days, 21 days and 40 days. I was privileged to be with him on a 7-day prayer and fasting at Oke-Ido Ajinare in 1932. I was there with him and some other persons. One sick man was with us on the mountain. We prayed for the man's healing for the first 5 days, nothing happened. On the 6th day Apostle Babalola said we should be thanking God for healing the man. It was on that day that the man got up and he was healed totally. Apostle Babalola was a man of faith indeed.

Also in 1948 at Oke-Lisa, Akure Apostle Babalola, the President of the laity Elder Oluwatuyi and my humble self fasted for 40 days non-stop. He was so used to fasting that many people thought he never ate food. He rarely ate in public. His favourite foods were pounded yam, fufu and pap.

More often than not, whenever we went on missionary journeys he would not eat for as many days as we spend there. Our hosts would just be packing their food untouched each night.

Whenever we travelled together we would pray at every stop on the journey. Prayer must be offered before any take—off even when we waited briefly to answer the call of nature.

He was a prayer warrior. He would pray all-night, all-day, on top of mountains and everywhere. Whenever his tight schedule permitted he used to pray to at the dot of every watch hour i.e. 6.00am, 9.00am, 12 noon, 3.00pm e.t.c. His prayers were usually fervent and ferocious.

2. ***Moses Oludele Idowu's Account:*** *Lets take another account of the prayer life of Joseph Ayo Babalola from the book MANTLE OF AN APOSTLE written by Moses Oludele Idowu.*

Price of prayer

> *And he spake a parable unto them to this end that man ought always to pray; and not faint Luke 18:1*

> *Pray without ceasing 1 Thessalonians 5:17*

These two scriptural passages may well summarize the life and ministry of Joseph Ayo Babalola. Prayer—and not preaching—was the main business and pursuit of his life. To say that he prayed was an understatement: he lived and breathed prayer.

The flame of prayer never died on his altar night and day. The oil of prayer was always on his life to lubricate the engine of God's supernatural power. This was the reason why the great power of God never departed from his life to the very end of his ministry. "Even when you are talking with him", said one of his associate to me: "he was praying in his heart to God"

He had an unbroken communion with God. He believed that there is prayer solution to every human or natural problem. As a result of this he was able to solve many unbelievable problems and provide incredible answers in the face of daunting needs and major crises. As busy as he was, he was never too busy to pray. Prayer was far more important to him than his necessary food. He was a great prayer warrior.

Says the daughter, Mrs Oginni:

"Baba was indeed a great prayer warrior and believed very much in the power of prayer. I believe most of his successes was due to this fact"

Frequently he would retire to the mountain for a period of sustained, concentrated, fervent and undisturbed prayer; and for days he would be there on his face in communion with God, His Maker, most of the time without food. They having received new grace and unction from the Almighty, he would descend again to minister same to the people over which the Holy Ghost had made him overseer.

C.   SUNDAY ADELAJA

For those unfamiliar with him, he pastors the biggest church in Ukraine, 20,000+ members, called the Embassy of God. He and his church members were prominent in Ukraine's Orange Revolution in late 2004, early 2005.[g]

The changes in Ukraine have a history. They were birthed in much prayer. In one message, Pastor Sunday told us how he spends one week out of every four in isolation, fasting and praying. This is to intercede for the country, the church and to get God's direction and strategy.

The Embassy of God sponsors a spring and a fall festival each year. These are ten to twelve-day stretches when up to 1000 people (from his church and from all over Europe—countries from the former Soviet Union, Holland, Germany etc.) will gather. There they will spend the entire time in fasting and prayer. They will pray up to ten hours at a stretch.

On Tuesday night, Pastor Sunday told us the story of how he learned to pray. (These are the exact words from his message—which I transcribed [see, I knew my medical transcription experience would prove valuable for some kingdom purpose!]).

In the words of Sunday Adelaja:

Now, anywhere you see a visitation, a genuine visitation, somebody has been found who stood in the gap. That's why I said, we prayed, not just some sweety-sweety prayer. We must learn to pray the kind of prayer that James was talking about, that, you know, the fervent prayer of the righteous cannot but avail much. It must bring results. It must produce the rain of righteousness.

In our church, you know, in Ukraine, when I went to the Ukraine in 1993, the first time when I went to visit, I was coming from Belarus. I started in Belarus. And when I entered Ukraine, where I am today, I felt like there was a dark cloud over the whole city, over the country. And I would say, "My, are there no churches in this city? Why is it so bad?" I could feel the heaviness. Maybe some people went to Russia in the '90s. In the early '90s. You could see the cloud. It was even worse than Belarus at that point.

Then I was walking the streets and I was praying, "Oh God, raise up men to pray this thing through." And I never knew a year later, God was going to send me there. So when God sent me there, I knew the first thing I needed to do was to pray through.

Now God had taught me to pray through while I was a student, just years before then, during communism. I was a student. There was no church. We couldn't have any relations with the underground church so we were just isolated on the campus, the student campus. And at the point when I knew I was giving up, I was defeated, I couldn't hold on any longer, communism was shrinking me and brothers and sisters who came as believers were all backsliding. You know, people were being sent to the psychiatric hospital, people were being sent to mental hospitals because they were Christians and others were leaving the country, and so when it was so difficult, there was another believer. We made a covenant and we said, "We are going to meet every day. No matter what we do. No matter where we go. No matter what happens. We are going to meet every day until God does something or heaven opens."

So we made a covenant with ourselves to meet together, not to talk, not to preach. Not to do anything else. Just to intercede and pray together for two hours minimum. Minimum from two, three, four.

That was the most difficult one year in my whole life. I could pray before then for two hours, but to do it every day? Everything fought it. My professors would ask me to come to class. I was a student, then, in the university. My classmates would come and you couldn't pray openly. You were being watched. You were being monitored. To find a place of isolation—oh yeah, my God, we needed to go through hell just to keep that covenant. But we did.

When it was one year, after we were praying two hours every single day, heaven broke loose. It was like we were no more under communism. The Spirit of God descended on us like mad. People began to get saved through us. God broke the chains and led us supernaturally to the believers, to the Russian believers in the underground church. We got a breakthrough. We began to fellowship together, preach together.

That was how my ministry began in 1991. The Holy Ghost began to appear. When I woke up in the morning, I would lie on my bed, cover myself and I just prayed one hour, straight in tongues, no English, no Russian, just wake up, and . . . (here he began praying in tongues to demonstrate and in the next 20 minutes or so, a fire of prayer swept through the room).

Note: At a National prayer breakfast prior to President Barrack Obama's 50th Birthday, the US president said prayer is his secret[h]

Hear him: "When I wake in the morning, I wait on the Lord, I ask him to give me the strength to do right by our country and our people."

"And when I go to bed at night, I wait on the Lord and I ask him to forgive me my sins and to look after my family and to make me an instrument of the Lord."—the president said at the National Prayer Breakfast.

TWENTY SEVEN

PRAYER SONGS/HYMNS

Spiritual songs and hymns play a prominent role in our prayers.

Colossians 3:16 Let the word of Christ dwell in you richly in all wisdom, teaching and admonishing one another in psalms and hymns and spiritual songs, singing with grace in your hearts to the Lord

There are several prayer songs/hymns, we just take few.

1. Prayer is the key (2ce)
   Prayer is the master key
   Jesus started with prayer
   And ended with prayer
   Prayer is the master key.

2. Call upon me in the day of trouble,
   call upon me and I will answer you

3. Spirit of the living God,
   Fall fresh on me.
   Spirit of the living God,
   Fall fresh on me.
   Break me! Mold me! Fill me!
   Spirit of the living God, fall on me.

4. I just ` want to be where you are . . . . Don Moen[a]

I just want to be where You are,
dwelling daily in Your presence
I don't want to worship from afar,
draw me near to where You are

I just want to be where You are,
in Your dwelling place forever
Take me to the place where You are,
I just want to be with You

Chorus
I want to be where You are,
dwelling in Your presence
Feasting at Your table,
surrounded by Your glory
In Your presence,
that's where I always want to be
I just want to be,
I just want to be with You

I just want to be where You are,
to enter boldly in Your presence
I don't want to worship from afar,
draw me near to where You are

Oh, my God,
You are my strength and my song
And when I'm in Your presence
Though I'm weak You're always strong

Ending
I just want to be
I just want to be with You

5. Lord you are more precious than silver
   Lord you are more costly than gold
   Lord you are more beautiful than diamonds
   And nothing I desire compares with you

6. **More Love, More power Songwriter: Jude Del Hierro**

   More love, more power
   More of You in my life
   More love, more power
   More of You in my life

   And I will worship You with all of my heart
   I will worship you with all of my mind
   I will worship you with all of my strength
   For You are my Lord

7. **I Stand in Awe** *by Mark Altrogge*

   You are beautiful beyond description,
   Too marvelous for words,
   Too wonderful for comprehension,
   Like nothing ever seen or heard.
   Who can grasp your infinite wisdom?
   Who can fathom the depth of your love?
   You are beautiful beyond description,
   Majesty enthroned above.

   (Chorus)
   And I stand, I stand in awe of you.
   I stand, I stand in awe of you.
   Holy God, to whom all praise is due,
   I stand in awe of you.

   You are beautiful beyond description,
   Yet God crushed You for my sin,
   In agony and deep affliction,
   Cut off that I might enter in.

Who can grasp such tender compassion?
Who can fathom this mercy so free?
You are beautiful beyond description,
Lamb of God, Who died for me.
(Chorus)

8. O the blood of Jesus (3x). It washes white as snow.

9. BREATH ON ME (2x), HOLY GHOST FIRE, BREATH ON ME, YESTERDAY IS GONE, TODAY I'M IN NEED, HOLY GHOST FIRE, BREATH ON ME

10. I CALL YOU HOLY, YOUR NAME IS HOLY, YOU ARE SO HOLY TO ME, I CALL YOU HOLY, YOUR NAME IS HOLY, HOLY YOU ARE AND HOLY YOU'LL BE

11. **Eagle's wings[b] Lyrics** from:

Here I am waiting, abide in me, I pray
Here I am longing for You
Hide me in Your love, bring me to my knees
May I know Jesus more and more

Come live in me all my life, take over
Come breathe in me, I will rise on eagle's wings
Come live in me all my life, take over
Come breathe in me, I will rise on eagle's wings

Here I am waiting, abide in me, I pray
Here I am longing for You
Hide me in Your love, bring me to my knees
May I know Jesus more and more

Come live in me all my life, take over
Come breathe in me, I will rise on eagle's wings
Come live in me all my life, take over
Come breathe in me, I will rise on eagle's wings

Come live in me all my life, take over
Come breathe in me, I will rise on eagle's wings
I will rise on eagle's wings, I will rise on eagle's wings
I will rise on eagle's wings, I will rise on eagle's wings

I will rise on eagle's wings, I will rise on eagle's wings
On eagle's wings

12. He is the mighty God, the great I am Haleluyah, haleluyah . . . .

13. Lord You Are Welcome written by Kurt Lykes

Lord, You are welcome in this place.
Lord, You are welcome in this place.
Lord You are welcome in this place,
have Your way.

Move by Your Spirit in this place.
Move by Your Spirit in this place.
Move by Your spirit in this place,
have Your way.

Send Your anointing in this place.
Send Your anointing in this place.
Send Your anointing in this place,
have Your way.

Heal and deliver in this place.
Heal and deliver in this place.
Heal and deliver in this place,
have Your way.

14. There is power mighty in the blood, there is power mighty in the blood, there is power mighty in the blood of Jesus Christ, there is power mighty in the blood.

15. Send down fire, holy ghost fire, send down fire again, Holy ghost fire.

16. The blood of Jesus, the blood of Jesus sets me free, from sins and sorrows, the blood of Jesus sets me free

17. You Are My All In All—Dennis Jernigan[c]

You are my strength when I am weak
You are the treasure that I seek
You are my all in all
Seeking You as a precious jewel
Lord, to give up I'd be a fool
You are my all in all

Jesus, Lamb of God
Worthy is Your name
Jesus, Lamb of God

Taking my sin, my cross, my shame
Rising again I bless Your name
You are my all in all
When I fall down You pick me up
When I am dry You fill my cup
You are my all in all

Jesus, Lamb of God
Worthy is Your name
Jesus, Lamb of God
Worthy is Your name

Oh my
Jesus, Lamb of God
Worthy is Your name
Jesus, Lamb of God
Worthy is Your

18. Holy Ghost do it again, do it again in my life, open my life, to see Jesus, seated upon the throne

19. Come Holy Spirit we need you
Come Holy Spirit we pray
Come in your strength and your power
Come in your own special way.

20. Our God is a great God, a great God above other gods

21. He has given me victory
I will lift Him higher
Jehovah, I will lift Him higher.

22. Israel & New Breed—Alpha And Omega

You are Alpha and Omega
We worship you our Lord
you are worthy to be praised
We give you all the glory
we worship you our Lord
you are worthy to be praised

23. Anointing fall on me . . . . Ron Kenoly.

Anointing fall on me
Anointing fall on me
Let the power
Of the Holy Ghost
Fall on me
Anointing fall on me

Touch my hands my mouth
And my heart
Fill my life Lord
Every part
Let the power
Of the Holy Ghost
Fall on me
Anointing fall on me

On me let the power
Of the Holy Ghost
Fall on me
Anointing fall on me
Anointing fall on me

24. Draw me close to you—Song Writer Kelly Roberts Carpenter

Draw me close to you, never let me go
I lay it all down again to hear you say that I'm your friend
You are my desire, no one else will do
'Cause nothing else can take your place
To feel the warmth of your embrace
Help me find the way, bring me back to you

You're all I want
You're all I've ever needed
You're all I want
Help me know you are near

Draw me close to you, never let me go
I lay it all down again to hear you say that I'm your friend
You are my desire, no one else will do
'Cause nothing else can take your place
To feel the warmth of your embrace
Help me find the way, bring me back to you

You're all I want
You're all I've ever needed
You're all I want
Help me know you are near

You're all I want
You're all I've ever needed
You're all I want
Help me know you are near
Help me know you are near
Help me know you are near

25. Order my steps in your word[d]

(Choir)
Order my steps in Your Word, Dear Lord
Lead me, guide me every day
Send Your anointing, Father, I pray
Order my steps in Your Word, YES
Order my steps in Your Word

(Lead)
Humbly I ask Thee, teach me Thy will
While You are working, I will keep still
Satan is busy, God is real
Order my steps in Your Word, YES
Order my steps in Your Word

Write on my tongue, let my words edify
Let the words of my mouth be acceptable in Thy sight
Take charge of my thoughts both day and night
Order my steps in Your Word, YES
Order my steps in Your Word

(Choir)
Order my steps in Your Word, Dear Lord
Lead me, guide me every day
Send Your anointing, Father, I pray
Order my steps in Your Word, YES
Order my steps in Your Word

I want to walk worthy, my calling to fulfill
Yes, order my steps Lord
And I'll do Your blessed will
The world is ever changing
But You are still the same
If You order my steps, I'll praise Your name

Order my steps in Your Word
Order my tongue in Your Word

Wash my heart in Your Word
Guide my feet in Your Word
Show me how to walk in Your Word
Show me how to talk in Your Word
Provide me a brand new song to sing
Show me how to let Your praises ring
In Your Word, in Your Word, YES
Order my steps in Your Word, YES
Order my steps in Your Word

(Choir)
Order my steps in Your Word, Dear Lord
Lead me, guide me every day
Send Your anointing, Father, I pray
Order my steps in Your Word, YES
Order my steps in Your Word

(Lead)
Humbly I ask Thee, teach me Thy will
While You are working, I will keep still
Satan is busy, God is real
Order my steps in Your Word, YES
Order my steps in Your Word

Write on my tongue, let my words edify
Let the words of my mouth be acceptable in Thy sight
Take charge of my thoughts both day and night
Order my steps in Your Word, YES
Order my steps in Your Word

(Choir)
Order my steps in Your Word, Dear Lord
Lead me, guide me every day
Send Your anointing, Father, I pray
Order my steps in Your Word, YES
Order my steps in Your Word

I want to walk worthy, my calling to fulfill
Yes, order my steps Lord
And I'll do Your blessed will
The world is ever changing
But You are still the same
If You order my steps, I'll praise Your name

Order my steps in Your Word
Order my tongue in Your Word
Wash my heart in Your Word
Guide my feet in Your Word
Show me how to walk in Your Word
Show me how to talk in Your Word
Provide me a brand new song to sing
Show me how to let Your praises ring
In Your Word, in Your Word, YES
Order my steps in Your Word, YES
Order my steps in Your Word

26. Ancient Words (Michael W. Smith)

Holy words long preserved
for our walk in this world,
They resound with God's own heart.
Oh let the ancient words impart

Words of Life, words of Hope
Give us strength, help us cope
In this world, where e'er we roam
Ancient words will guide us Home.

CHORUS:
Ancient words ever true
Changing me and changing you,
We have come with open hearts
Oh let the ancient words impart

Holy words of our Faith
Handed down to this age
Came to us through sacrifice
Oh heed the faithful words of Christ.

Holy words long preserved
For our walk in this world.
They resound with God's own heart
Oh let the ancient words impart.

CHORUS x4
We have come with open hearts
Oh let the ancient words impart

27. MORE OF YOU—Sinach [e]

Chorus
I want more of you
I want more of you Jesus
Cause the more I know you
The more I want to know you
Jesus More of you
Solo
You make my life so beautiful
As you are you have made me on earth
There's nothing greater than this
That is why I will love you evermore
Ref
More of you
More of you
More of you
Jesus more of you

28. AWESOME GOD—Sinach [f]

Holy are you Lord
All creation call you God
Worthy is your name

We worship Your Majesty
Awesome God, how great thou art
You are God, mighty are Your miracles
We stand in awe of your holy name
Lord we bow and worship You
King of kings, Lord of lords, everlasting Kind
Savior Redeemer, Soon coming King
King of kings, Lord of lords, everlasting Kind
Savior Redeemer, Soon coming King
Awesome, awesome, You are awesome
Awesome, awesome, You are awesome
. . . . X
Awesome is your name.

29. What a Friend we have in Jesus, all our sins and grief to bear!
What a privilege to carry everything to God in prayer!
O what peace we often forfeit, O what needless pain we bear,
All because we do not carry everything to God in prayer.

Have we trials and temptations? Is there trouble anywhere?
We should never be discouraged; take it to the Lord in prayer.
Can we find a friend so faithful who will all our sorrows share?
Jesus knows our every weakness; take it to the Lord in prayer.

Are we weak and heavy laden, cumbered with a load of care?
Precious Savior, still our refuge, take it to the Lord in prayer.
Do your friends despise, forsake you? Take it to the Lord in prayer!
In His arms He'll take and shield you; you will find a solace there.

Blessed Savior, Thou hast promised Thou wilt all our burdens bear
May we ever, Lord, be bringing all to Thee in earnest prayer.
Soon in glory bright unclouded there will be no need for prayer
Rapture, praise and endless worship will be our sweet portion there.

30. I need Thee every hour, most gracious Lord;
No tender voice like Thine can peace afford.

Refrain

I need Thee, O I need Thee;
Every hour I need Thee;
O bless me now, my Savior,
I come to Thee.

I need Thee every hour, stay Thou nearby;
Temptations lose their power when Thou art nigh.

Refrain

I need Thee every hour, in joy or pain;
Come quickly and abide, or life is in vain.

Refrain

I need Thee every hour; teach me Thy will;
And Thy rich promises in me fulfill.

Refrain

I need Thee every hour, most Holy One;
O make me Thine indeed, Thou blessèd Son.

31. Christian! seek not yet repose,
Hear thy guardian angel say;
Thou art in the midst of foes;
Watch and pray.

Principalities and powers,
Mustering their unseen array,
Wait for thy unguarded hours;
Watch and pray.

Gird thy heavenly armor on,
Wear it ever night and day;
Ambushed lies the evil one;
Watch and pray.

Hear the victors who o'
ercame;
Still they mark each warriors way;
All with one clear voice exclaim,
Watch and pray.

Hear, above all, hear thy Lord,
Him thou lovest to obey;
Hide within thy heart His Word,
Watch and pray.

Watch, as if on that alone
Hung the issue of the day;
Pray that help may be sent down;
Watch and pray.

32. Nearer, my God, to Thee, nearer to Thee!
E'en though it be a cross that raiseth me,
Still all my song shall be, nearer, my God, to Thee.

Refrain

Nearer, my God, to Thee,
Nearer to Thee!

Though like the wanderer, the sun gone down,
Darkness be over me, my rest a stone.
Yet in my dreams I'd be nearer, my God to Thee.

Refrain

There let the way appear, steps unto Heav'n;
All that Thou sendest me, in mercy given;

Angels to beckon me nearer, my God, to Thee.

Refrain

Then, with my waking thoughts bright with Thy praise,
Out of my stony grief s Bethel I'll raise;
So by my woes to be nearer, my God, to Thee.

Refrain

Or, if on joyful wing cleaving the sky,
Sun, moon, and stars forgot, upward I'll fly,
Still all my song shall be, nearer, my God, to Thee.

Refrain

There in my Father's home, safe and at rest,
There in my Savior's love, perfectly blest;
Age after age to be, nearer my God to Thee.

Refrain

33. Pray always pray;
the Holy Spirit pleads
Within thee all thy daily,
hourly needs.

Pray always pray;
beneath sin's heaviest load
Prayer sees the blood
from Jesus' side that flowed.

Pray always pray;
though weary faint, and lone,
Prayer nestles by
the Father's shelt'ring throne.

Pray always pray;
amid the world's turmoil
Prayer keeps the heart at rest,
and nerves for toil

Pray always pray;
if joys thy pathway throng,
Prayer strikes the harp,
and sings the angels' song.

Pray always pray;
if loved ones pass the veil
Prayer drinks with them
of springs that cannot fail.

All earthly things
with earth shall fade away;
Prayer grasps eternity:
pray, always pray.

34. Pass me not, O gentle Savior,
Hear my humble cry;
While on others Thou art calling,
Do not pass me by.

Refrain:
Savior, Savior,
Hear my humble cry,
While on others Thou are calling,
Do not pass me by.

Let me at a throne of mercy
Find a sweet relief;
Kneeling there in deep contrition,
Help my unbelief.

Trusting only in Thy merit,
Would I seek Thy face;

Heal my wounded, broken spirit,
Save me by Thy grace.

Thou the spring of all my comfort,
More than life to me,
Whom have I on earth beside Thee,
Whom in Heav'n but Thee.

35. I come to the garden alone
While the dew is still on the roses
And the voice I hear falling on my ear
The Son of God discloses.

Refrain:
And He walks with me, and He talks with me,
And He tells me I am His own;
And the joy we share as we tarry there,
None other has ever known.

He speaks, and the sound of His voice,
Is so sweet the birds hush their singing,
And the melody that He gave to me
Within my heart is ringing.

I'd stay in the garden with Him
Though the night around me be falling,
But He bids me go; through the voice of woe
His voice to me is calling.

36. God sent His Son, they called Him Jesus
He came to love, heal, and forgive
He lived and died to buy my pardon
An empty grave is there to prove my Saviour lives.

Because He lives I can face tomorrow
Because He lives all fear is gone
Because I know He holds the future
And life is worth the living just because He lives.

How sweet to hold a new born baby
And feel the pride, a joy he gives
But greater still the calm assurance
This child can face uncertain days because He lives.

And then one day I'll cross the river
I'll fight life's final war with pain
And then as death gives way to vict'ry
I'll see the lights of glory and I'll know He lives.

37. From every stormy wind that blows,
from every swelling tide of woes,
There is a calm, a sure retreat:
'Tis found beneath the mercy seat.

There is a place where Jesus sheds
the oil of gladness on our heads,
A place than all besides more sweet;
it is the bloodstained mercy seat.

There is a spot where spirits blend,
where friend holds fellowship with friend.
Tho' sundered far; by faith they meet
around the common mercy seat.

Ah, whither could we flee for aid,
when tempted, desolate, dismayed,
Or how the hosts of hell defeat,
had suffering saints no mercy seat.

There, there on eagle wings we soar
and time and sense seem all not more,
and heav'n comes down our souls to greet,
and glory crowns the mercy seat.

38. Lots more.

TWENTY EIGHT

EXAMPLES OF PRAYER POINTS
DEVELOPMENT

When starting out with prayers, it is expedient you write out your points. This helps to stay focused, avoid praying aimlessly and prevent drifting or being empty during prayers.

- One of the ways to develop prayers points is to be a student of the word of God. You must know what God is saying about the subject you want to pray about. Learn to pray the scriptures and personalize it.

  Colossians 3:16 Let the word of Christ dwell in you richly in all wisdom, teaching and admonishing one another in psalms and hymns and spiritual songs, singing with grace in your hearts to the Lord.

- Another way is through the Holy Spirit. Romans 8:28. Many people pray general prayers, but the Holy Spirit helps you to pray specifically about an issue.

  <u>Example:</u> When David discovered that Ahithophel was part of the conspiracy against him, he just prayed an heart-felt prayer.

  2 Samuel 15:31 Then someone told David saying "Ahithophel is among the conspirators with Absalom." And David said, "O LORD, I pray, turn the counsel of Ahithophel into foolishness!"

- Others are natural knowledge in the area of the issue, experience, exposure, education, etc. Know how to analyze a problem

  Proverbs 11:9b . . . But through knowledge the righteous will be delivered

- Lots more.

We would pick some topics and list some of its likely prayer points. The list is inexhautive. You may develop more on your own

A.   PROSPERITY, BLESSINGS

1. Oh Lord, Bless me indeed—*1 Chronicles 4:9-10*
2. Oh Lord, Bless the work of my hands and empower me to prosper *Psalm 90:17, Deut 8:18*
3. Oh Lord Give me uncommon blessings *Deut 28:1-13*
4. Oh Lord Give me extended blessings *Deut 15:6*
5. Oh Lord Give me what money can buy and much more what money cannot buy.
6. Oh Lord, send helpers my way and open doors for me. *Revelation 3:8*
7. Oh Lord grant me favour and mercy before decision makers (kings, judges, CEOs, Principals, Facilitators, Security personals, etc) *Genesis 43:14.*
8. Oh Lord Do not let me misuse your blessings. Let me still behave normal when you bless me. *Ps 62:10*
9. Oh Lord Bless me and make me a source of blessings. Make my life very fruitful *Gen 12:1-3*
10. Oh Lord Let there be progressive increase in every area of my life. *Psalm 115:14, Psalm 71:21*
11. Oh Lord Turn my pains into gains, turn my tests into triumphs, weaknesses into strength, tears into joy, etc *Ps 30:12*
12. Lots more—*Deut 1:11, Deut 28:1-14, Ps 23:1.*

B. <u>ENEMIES</u>

1. Oh Lord, Make me stronger than my enemies.
2. Oh Lord, Don't let me fall into the hands of my enemies. Make my enemies my foot stool.
3. Oh Lord, Do not let my enemy rejoice over me. Do not let my enemy recover.
4. Oh Lord, Deliver me from the traps, strategies, schemes of my enemies.
5. Oh Lord, Let me see my desire on my enemies.
6. Oh Lord, Guide my enemies in the wrong path. *2 Samuel 17:17-20.* Turn the plans of my enemies into foolishness. *2 Sam 15:31.*
7. Oh Lord, Stop and reverse every workings of the enemies in my life *Zech 3:2*
8. Heavenly father, Give me strength over all levels of the enemies (*Ephesians 6:12*—i. Principalities ii. Powers iii. Rulers of darkness iv. Spiritual hosts of wickedness)
9. Oh Lord, be an enemy to all my enemies. Do not let me be my own enemy. *Exodus 23:22.*
10. Almighty God, Give me strength to pull down strong holds *2 Corn 10:4-6*
11. All powerful God, Destroy and execute judgment on all my enemies by fire, the blood, stones, sword, earthquakes, tsunami, death, etc *Exodus 12:12-13*
12. Lots more *Isaiah 54:17, Deut 28:7, psalm 64:2, Psalm 66:3.*

C. <u>DELIVERANCE</u>

1. Eternal rocks of ages, visit the foundation of my problems with earthquake and tsunami. visit the source of my problems *Psalm 11:3*
2. Unquestionable God, Stop all the works of darkness in my life. *Psalm 7:9a*
3. Deliver me from all my strong enemies. Deliver me from the captivity of the mighty. *Isaiah 49:24-25.*
4. Set me free from all bondages and shackles of life.
5. Uproot all evil plans in my life

6. Train my hands to war
7. Pull me out of the miry clay. Bear me up on eagles wings
8. All Knowing God, Instruct me on what I need to do.
9. Deliver me from all evil *2 Timothy 4:8*
10. Don't let me fall into the hands of the evil ones
11. Deliver me by fire, wipe away my tears
12. Lots more—*Psalm 18, 118, 27, 91.*

D. CAREERS, CALLINGS, JOBS, POSITION, ENTERPRISE

1. Show me what I am crafted for *Jeremiah 1:9-10*
2. Let my gifts, talents, training, etc make a way for me *Proverbs 18:16*
3. Let me get to the best of heights in my pursuit
4. Bring me in contact with people that are godly and have wise counsels (mentors, coaches, trainers, facilitators, etc) that will show me the way
5. Let me stand before kings and make me be an authority in my field. *Proverbs 22:29*
6. Lead me to where I am most needed
7. Help me to solve problems for people and help me to meet the needs of people.
8. Don't give me what I cannot handle. Don't give me what will destroy me *Psalm 106:15*. MAKE me (*Luke 15:19*) before GIVING me (*Luke 15:12*).,
9. Don't let someone else take my labours. Don't let me be edged out when it is time to reap
10. Help me to be wise and discerning in heart. *Genesis 41:39*
11. Don't let me be busy in the wrong direction
12. Lots more.

E. HEALTH, HEALING

1. Forgive all my sins and heal all my diseases *Psalm 103:2*
2. Take sickness away from me-*Deut 7:15, Exodus 23:25-26*

3. Teach me what to eat, where to eat, and when to eat and how to eat.
4. The blood of Jesus flow in my body and cleanse my body, soul and spirit from all impurities
5. By His stripes I am healed *1 Peter 2:24*
6. The Spirit that raised up Jesus will quicken my mortal body *Roman 8:11*
7. Preserve my spirit, soul and body
8. My natural strength will not abate *Deut 34:7*
9. Teach me deep things that pertain to life and godliness
10. Every arrow of sickness fired against me will not prosper and go back to sender *Isaiah 54:17*
11. The joy of the Lord is my strength. The Lord will renew my strength. *Nehemiah 8:10, Isaiah 40:30-31*
12. Lots more.

F. PERSONAL COMMITMENT TO GOD

1. Lord, I offer my life to you, use me for your glory
2. Let me love what you love
3. Let me hate what you hate
4. Let me please you
5. Reshape me into what is fit for You. *Jeremiah 18:1-10*
6. Don't look at my sins and have mercy on me.
7. Let me fear you
8. Purify and purge my life by fire. *Malachi 3:2-3, Matthew 3:10-11*
9. Create in me a clean heart *Psalm 51:10*
10. Burn off all chaff and impurity in my life *Psalm 139:23-24*
11. May Christ be formed in my life
12. Lots more.

G. FORGIVENESS, CONFESSION

1. Lord, I am sorry for all my sins (*make a list and mention all—Spend quality time in prayer, might involve fasting*).
2. Lord, I confess my sins and the sins of my fathers, have mercy.

3. Don't cast me from your presence, O Lord.
4. Give me the grace to sin no more.
5. Don't leave me in my weakness.
6. I am not coming to you in my righteousness but in your GREAT MERCY.
7. I hand over all the sins of past and present to you. I don't need it anymore
8. Teach me how to walk in righteousness.
9. Reverse all the curses in my life (both the ones known to me and the ones unknown to me).
10. Restore all I have lost to carelessness and ignorance
11. I am running to you with my weaknesses, lapses, sins, iniquities, etc. Please help out.
12. Lots more.

H. RELATIONSHIPS

Blessings (promotion, contracts, success, breakthroughs, business, jobs, etc) flow through relationships

Curses (demotion, breakdown, failure, diseases, etc) also flow through relationships.

1. Bring wise and godly people my way. *Proverbs 13:20*
2. Cut off all evil people from my circle of influence *Psalm 28:3*
3. Help me to be the right person (Spend quality time)
4. Help me to link up with the right people in the following areas marriage, work, politics, business, schools (list more areas of interest)
5. Help me to keep quiet and not to speak more than necessary when wicked people are around. *Psalm 39:1*
6. Don't let me move with people (group, team, network, etc) that are destined for destruction.
7. Let the right people remember me. Send me help from ABOVE, help from ABROAD and raise helpers AROUND me.
8. Connect me to people that matter.
9. Reveal and expose everyone with hidden agenda around me. Reveal to me my true enemies and my false friends.

10. Purge all my relationships with fire
11. Help me to develop into someone of relevance that people will like to relate with.
12. Lots more.

I. <u>NEXT LEVEL (PROMOTION, UPLIFTMENT)</u>

1. Show me how to position myself (Natural and Spiritual)
2. Show me what I need to learn and commit to heart
3. Show me what I need to unlearn and put away
4. Make my latter end increase *Job 8:7*. Take me from one glory to another *2 Corinthians 3:18*
5. Make my path shine brighter and brighter *Proverbs 4:18*
6. Hold me and keep me from falling *1 Corinthians 15:58, Phi 1:6*
7. Show me what to do per time
8. Give me the grace to trust you when I am weary of waiting *Proverbs 13:12*
9. Set my feet on high, establish my goings
10. Don't let my past mar my future. HAVE MERCY.
11. Lead me to the rock that is higher than I. *Psalm 61:2*
12. Lots more. *Psalm 78:70-72.*

J. <u>BEFORE SAYING 'I DO' (MARRIAGE)</u>

1. Make me a good partner (either a good husband or good wife). *It might take months or years of prayer time*
2. Help me in all my weaknesses and make me strong in my weak areas. (*list them and pray them away. It may require deliberate efforts too*)
3. Grant me parental consent or approval and let me have peace with all my in-laws.
4. Give me the grace to know or recognize who is meant for my life and destiny
5. Give me favour Oh Lord *Proverbs 18:22*
6. Don't let me listen to the voice of strangers. *John 10:5, Isaiah 30:21*

7. Don't let me make the mistake of taking a wrong decision when choosing.
8. Choose your own person for me. Your perfect will. Bring my husband/Wife.
9. Separate me from all strange wife/husband
10. Let the blessings of marriage be within my reach(financial boom, fruit of the womb, joy, love, peace, etc)
11. Prepare me for the task ahead (spiritual, mental, financial, medical, and social) Let me marry at the right time. Let me marry well.
12. Lots more.

TWENTY NINE

QUESTIONS ON PRAYERS
(PERSONAL)

In order to make prayers simple, there might be a need to ask personal questions and to do an evaluation of where you are currently and where you have been and where you want to be. A 360 degree evaluation.

2 Corinthians 12:5 Examine yourselves as to whether you are in the faith. Test yourselves. Do you not know yourselves, that Jesus Christ is in you?—unless indeed you are disqualified.

The questions below is just a guide, you may add other personal questions as deem fit by your evaluation

1. Do you have a prayer life? Yes/No

2. How do you rate your prayer life? Excellent, Good, Can be better, Average, Poor

3. Is your prayer life consistent? Yes/No

4. When last did you actually pray? . . . .

5. What are the natural tools that can aid your prayer life?

. . .

6. What is stopping you or hindering you from praying consistently? Procrastination, Computer, Television, Internet, Indifference, Friends, laziness, Too Busy, Sin, Lack of Knowledge about prayers, Mention others

7. Do you belong to any prayer group, Network, or cell?

8. Do you keep prayer records and prayer list?

9. Do you keep record of answered prayers from God so you can be thankful?

10. Do you have specific time for prayers or pray at random?

11. Which prayer maintenance culture do you practice mostly?

12. Who do you call when you have prayer issues? . . . .

13. What spiritual tools can aid your prayer life?

. . .

14. When was the last time you attended a prayer conference, Prayer vigil, Prayer meeting, etc? . . . .

15. When was the last time you read or studied a book or audio material about prayer? . . . .

16. What prayer postures suits you most? . . . .

17. How often to you add fasting to your prayer life?

18. If married, do you pray with your partner?

19. If intending to get married. Have you been praying together with your intended?

20. Do you pray for your spiritual leaders? YES? NO

21. Do you pray for your political leaders? YES/NO

22. Do you pray for the spread of God's kingdom?

23. Do you pray for the peace of your country?

24. What work (preparation, training, skills development or virtues) should you engage in to balance your prayer life?

25. How do you hear from God after prayers?

. . .

26. How often do you obey instructions God gives after prayers

. . .

27. Do you need a prayer mentor to improve?

28. Do I seek God in prayers before major decisions (marriage, business, careers, close associates, etc)

29. Do you need to join prayer cells

30. Ask your questions

31. Ask your questions

32. Ask your questions

If you desire more information or clarification on any of the above, send a mail to prayersimplified@gmail.com

THIRTY

PRAYER CLOSET

(PRAYER RETREAT)

A man is as strong as other strong men around him. But more importantly, a man is as strong in the OPEN as he is in his CLOSET.

1. There is a time for every purpose *Ecclesiastes 3:1*

2. There is a time to shut down the television and phone

3. There is a time to shut down the computer system and the internet

4. There is a time to shut your door *Matthew 6:6*

5. There is a time to pull aside before taking a major decision

6. There is a time to separate from your family and friends in order to serve them better

7. There is a time to suspend sleep and take hold of the future *Genesis 32:24-27*

8. There is a time to deal with lingering and embarrassing issues *1 Samuel 1:10-11*

9. There is a time you need divine refilling and be strengthen *Luke 22:42, Ephesians 3:16*

10. There is a time to bear more fruit and move to the next level *John 15:5, Psalm 84:7*

11. There is a time your spirit, soul and body needs to be refreshed *Psalm 16:11*

12. There is a time to get divine ideas and revelations *Daniel 2: 19*

13. There is a time to just be with Him *John 15: 4*

14. There is a time to have spiritual evaluation of your life *2 Corinthians 13:5*

15. There is a time to be divinely instructed *Psalm 32:8*

16. There is a time to be divinely assured *Isaiah 43:2*

17. There is a time to be in the secret place *Psalm 91*

18. At a time you are burnt out or almost burning out *1 Kings 19:3*

19. At a time you need to exchange your weakness for His strength *2 Corinthians 12:8-9*

20. At a time when you are overwhelmed and you want to call it quit with your assignment *1 kings 19:2-18, Psalm 61:2*

21. At a time you need to clear all doubts *Luke 22:42-43*

22. It is a time to move from the natural into the supernatural

23. It is a time to run to the throne of grace *Hebrews 4:16*

24. It could be a time to move away from your normal environment *Exodus 19:3*

25. It could be a time to weep for your sins, sins of your forebears and sins of the nation *Daniel 9: 20*

26. It is a time to pull down resources from above

27. It is a time to pour out your heart to Him

28. Sometimes you do not have to say much . . . just listen *John 10:27, Isaiah 30:21*

29. It is a time to be alone with God *Jeremiah 29:12-13.*

30. It is a time to have a prayer retreat or enter into your closet

31. THAT TIME IS UP TO YOU TO DECIDE.

    This song can used in your closet (I COME TO THE GARDEN ALONE) BY <u>C. Austin Miles,</u>

    I come to the garden alone
    While the dew is still on the roses
    And the voice I hear falling on my ear
    The Son of God discloses.

    Refrain

    And He walks with me, and He talks with me,
    And He tells me I am His own;
    And the joy we share as we tarry there,
    None other has ever known

    Refrain

    He speaks, and the sound of His voice,
    Is so sweet the birds hush their singing,
    And the melody that He gave to me
    Within my heart is ringing.

    Refrain

I'd stay in the garden with Him
Though the night around me be falling,
But He bids me go; through the voice of woe
His voice to me is calling.

Refrain

REFERENCES

ONE

    a. *See Kathryn Kuhlman LORD TEACH US TO PRAY 1988 page 16, 18-19.*

EIGHT

    a. See Tim Lahaye, SPIRIT CONTROLLED TEMPERAMENT http://files.tyndale.com/thpdata/FirstChapters/978-0-8423-6220-7.pdf, https://timlahaye.com/shopdisplayproducts.asp?id=22&cat=TEMPERAMENT

NINE

    a. See R. Kent Hughes, 10th Anniversary edition 2001:DISCIPLINES OF A GODLY MAN Chapter 7, page 102,

EIGHTEEN

    a. See Don Fleming, *WORLD'S BIBLE DICTIONARY 1990 page 99*
    b. See Don Fleming, *WORLD'S BIBLE DICTIONARY 1990 page 453*
    c. See DICTIONARY OF DREAMS by Tella Olayeri 2009
    d. See Charles and Frances Hunter, *ANGELS ON ASSIGNMENT 1979 Chapter 2 page 19*
        For more about pastor Roland Buck and angelic messages online, visit www.angelsonassignment.org and http://angelsonassignment.org/sequel/index.html

TWENTY FOUR

a. See *Sunday Adelaja, CHURCH SHIFT 2008 Chapter 11 pages 150-151*

TWENTY SIX

a. Smith Wigglesworth, GOD'S GENERAL by Roberts Liardon 1996 pages 197-224
b. "PIONEERS OF FAITH" By Dr. Lester Sumrall 1995 page 165
c. "PIONEERS OF FAITH" By Dr. Lester Sumrall 1995 page 172
d. http://teamjesus.lifegroups.net/topic/58-a-story-about-smith-wigglesworths-prayer-life/ *Jeff in his blog, Mar 28 2011 11:39 PM*
e. http://www.sadela.org/babalola.htm Rev S.A Sadela, President/Founder, Gospel Apostolic Church 10th October 2008.
f. See Moses Oludele Idowu: JOSEPH AYO BABALOLA: MANTLE OF AN APOSTLE, Artillery publication pages 88-90
g. http://the-kingdom.blogspot.com/2006/10/sunday-adelaja-how-i-learned-to-pray.html
   The preceding narrative was transcribed by Violet Nesdoly at Christian Life Assembly, Langley, B.C., Canada in September, 2005, when Pastor Sunday was speaking at the church. Used with permission.
h. Fresh from debt ceiling success, Obama celebrates 50th birthday By Emma Emeozor Thursday, August 04, 2011 Daily Sun http://www.sunnewsonline.com/webpages/news/national/2011/aug/04/national-04-08-2011-07.html

TWENTY SEVEN

a. www.allthelyrics.com/lyrics/don_moen/
b. http://www.lyricsmode.com/lyrics/h/hillsong/eagles_wings.html
c. http://www.lyricsmode.com/lyrics/d/dennis_jernigan/you_are_my_all_in_all.html
d. http://www.lyricsmania.com/order_my_steps_lyrics_gmwa_women_of_worship.html
e. http://www.christembassy.org/music/sinach/lyrics.html
f. http://www.christembassy.org/music/sinach/lyrics.html

ALSO BY THE AUTHOR

LAYING A STRONG FOUNDATION IN CHRIST

The foundation (underground structure) of any set up is paramount to the sustenance and continuation of the body. However, it is disheartening to see a large number attend to altar calls and Christian gatherings only for a sizeable number to return to their previous ways. Even the 'standing believer' is not living the spiritual life to the full, hence this booklet is written.